The Collected and Recollected

The Collected and Recollected

Edited by Mark Amory
with an
Introduction by Craig Brown

FOURTH ESTATE · *London*

Introduction by Craig Brown

I get the feeling that Mark's old friends tended to pooh pooh the years he spent, towards the end of his life, editing *Tatler*. Yet it seems to me that it was a post beautifully matched to his character, and that he somehow managed to turn *Tatler* into a neat and witty reflection of the contradictions within his own personality.

Only those who hold themselves aloof from real life could imagine that Mark's caricatures, for all their beauty of line and spikiness of insight, could spring from a mind immune to fripperies. I remember him telling me that once he had got someone's hair right, the rest of their face tended to fall into place. Certainly, a great many of the subjects caricatured in this book – Lord Lambton, Paul Foot, Kenneth Baker, Arthur Koestler, Philip Roth – might be identified from their hair alone; others – Ian Paisley, Hugh Fraser, the Duke of Kent – from their ears; and still others – Gerald Kaufmann, Tom Stoppard, Terence Conran, Bubbles Rothermere (and how!) – from their clothes. 'I can never bring you to realise,' says Sherlock Holmes in 'A Case of Identity', 'the importance of sleeves, the suggestiveness of fingernails, or the great issues that may hang from a bootlace.'

Mark's art fed off his absorption in, and his ambivalence towards, high society. He was seen as a great party-goer, yet he confessed to a mutual friend that he would often find himself walking around the block three times before plucking up the courage to enter a party. He was once very sulky with me for going to interview Margaret, Duchess of Argyll without wearing a tie, yet his caricature of her – the eyes so black and as ungiving as a goat's, the eyelashes like dead spiders, the distended gash of a mouth – must have been far more alarming to Her Grace than the sight of a shabby journalist not wearing a tie. Similarly, when editing *Tatler* Mark was extraordinarily keen to get names and titles exactly right – inquisitions would be held over even the tiniest mistake – yet, as long as the name and the title were dead on, he would giggle with delight at the mischief and malice one might have poured over the correctly titled victim.

I have often thought that the puns which infected the headlines of Mark's *Tatler* represented a further outpost of this creative ambivalence, for a pun is schizophrenic, meaning two or more things at any single time, one straight, sophisticated, even snobbish, the other jam-packed with diablerie. When we were thinking of a title for a little piece on a dispute within the ranks of the Belvoir Hunt, someone came up with 'Split Belvoir'. Mark howled with laughter – his laugh sounded like a soda syphon out of control – and put it straight in.

He adored gossip, sometimes becoming so absorbed in it that it would backfire in his face. With Noel Annan and one or two others, he was once discussing which of their Cambridge contemporaries had not fulfilled his early promise. So carried away did Mark become with adding to the list that he momentarily forgot who he was talking to, saying 'and Noel Annan, of course!' But he was, by and large, only interested in gossiping about those whom he in some way admired. At one of our regular *Tatler* ideas meetings, someone suggested a profile of Lord Hanson. Mark despatched it in two seconds: 'No point. Nothing to him. A lot of people make the mistake of thinking him interesting, but the only thing he's ever done is to be engaged to Ava Gardner.'

He seemed particularly drawn to all gossip about his old employer and friend Lord Weidenfeld, for whom his fascination was unending, so much so that he once said to me that, were he ever to write a biography, he would choose Weidenfeld as his subject. He was mesmerised by Weidenfeld's social success combined with his occasional revelatory *faux pas* in which the feet of clay poked out of the embroidered socks. Perhaps somewhere inside him Mark saw Weidenfeld as a larger-than-life caricature of himself.

In the *Tatler* of December 1987, there was a profile of Weidenfeld, printed under the punning heading – perfect from every angle – 'Publish and Be Grand'. It was written pseudonymously, and perhaps by several hands, but had one anecdote in it that seemed pure Mark: 'At one time, Geoffrey Keating, the Mr Fixit of his generation, used to attend Weidenfeld's gatherings as a matter of course. He fell from grace. It was explained that he was to come no more. Wandering alone one evening he spotted Harold Wilson, then Prime Minister, with his wife, and it emerged that Harold was busy but would be grateful if Keating could escort Mary to that evening's party. As Weidenfeld opened the door, his face darkened and he began, "I thought I had made it quite clear, and who is this woman?"'

Like that other great English caricaturist, Max Beerbohm (also a dandy), Mark delighted in the telling detail, the glint on the exterior that betrayed the presence of the weapons beneath. Transformed by Mark's pen, John Aspinall, for all his smart black tie, benevolent smile and frilly shirt, has the hairy hand of a gorilla emerging from his cuffs; Sir Hugh Casson has tiny little sparkles emerging from his eyes; Antonia Fraser sports a crucifix around her neck and a love-heart around her wrist; Lord Weidenfeld, with tiny little feet, has eyes at right angles to one another ('For an instant, as you enter his drawing-room, it is you that George Weidenfeld is looking at over someone else's shoulder' began the *Tatler* profile); and Lord Longford's head becomes curiously phallic (giving a new twist to Malcolm Muggeridge's remark that 'Frank is almost *passionately* bald'). Mark relished the juxtaposition of the base and the suave: his skill relied upon the exact balancing of the two, so that the base instinct and the suave pretence became companions, dependent yet at odds, at one and the same time.

After a visit to the opera the night before, Mark came into the *Tatler* office full of excitement and related a piece of gossip that was the equivalent of the gorilla hand of Aspinall. A few weeks before, he had been chatting to a dermatologist at a party. The dermatologist had told him of a new method of hair replacement which involved planting the patient's pubic hair on the bald patch. He told Mark that a senior Tory politician was undergoing this treatment, but professional discretion forbade him from revealing which one. At the opera, Mark found that the head behind which he sat belonged to Mr (as he then was) Norman St John Stevas. With his eye for hair, Mark had studied it carefully, and had arrived at the only possible conclusion: pubic hair on a politician's head at Covent Garden! His joy was unconfined.

Mark aspired to worldliness, yet happily his sense of fun kept diverting him from that fateful course. In the office, he would occasionally try to be Machiavellian, but was always too innocent − almost gauche − to pull it off, hooting with laughter when the person he was plotting against made a joke, and consequently forgetting that any plot was underway. He never sacked anyone, however hard he tried.

Mark was a sort of Peter Pan figure, and with some of the vanity and petulance of Peter too. While his contemporaries may have seen his decision to take on *Tatler* as a sign of his continued immaturity, I believe that in actual fact it allowed him to grow up without shedding his youthfulness. He developed a paternal streak towards his staff, most of whom were about half his age, egging them on to better things (even if it meant leaving *Tatler*) and encouraging them to experiment, and to write with greater idiosyncrasy. Many of those who worked on *Tatler* owe him their future careers, the present editors of *Harpers & Queen*, *Mademoiselle* and *Vogue* among us. He had a zest, a capacity for delight that precluded not only the smug but also the hackish. I find it hard to think of anyone else who crackled with such life. It doesn't surprise me that two who knew him far better than I did − George Melly and Martin Amis − both recall in these pages how they have found themselves dreaming that he is still alive. Even now, five years after his death, I half expect that when I walk into a London party Mark will greet me with a big smile, tell me − a little brutally − that I am spreading my writing too thin, temper this by congratulating me on something-or-other, and then hiss with glee at some new piece of gossip. And if I have not seen him at a party for all these years, I still feel that he is there floating above us all, pen in hand, his half-moon glasses way down his nose, his eyes peering over us, intent, meticulous, concentrated, ready to re-create the fluffed-up feathers, the colourful plumes and the absurd chirrupings of the assembled company, like a divine bird-watcher rejoicing in his prey.

Magdalen, deer park, president's garden
and New buildings

Rosemary Sayigh

Father spent most of the year that Mark was born levelling out a tennis court in the garden of the house we lived in then at Chorleywood. It was 1931 and he had lost his job selling tractors to Latin America. That same summer Mother's West Highland White terriers produced a litter, a basket of pups that figure in the first photo of Mark. He is a few weeks old, just home from the nursing home, held by a temporary nanny. Pedigreed, the pups were probably a way of making extra income, the first of many of Mother's schemes. The nanny, the pedigree dogs, Mark's cashmere christening shawl all belong to the brief beginnings of our parents' marriage, a niche from which they were gradually squeezed out.

World recession and decline of empire hit both Mother's and Father's families. The year of Mark's birth Father's youngest brother put his head in a gas oven, while one of Mother's sisters, whose husband had lost his job in India, tried to abort by throwing herself downstairs. It is stories like these that form my earliest memories, not the temporary trappings of upper-middle classishness that show up in the first pages of our family photo album. Soon the Chorleywood house was sold so that Father could start his own secondhand car business in Watford. We moved into half a council house in a village called Sarratt. The other half was occupied by the owners, 'Flinty' and her chauffeur husband. Flinty housekept while Mother went off all week lecturing to school children for the Dental Board.

Mother and Father came from similar backgrounds, middle-class professional people descended from farmers and tradesmen who had migrated to London from the provinces early in the nineteenth century. On both sides there had been men of achievement; a great-uncle of Mother's was the early neurologist Charles Hughlings Jackson; Father's great-grandfather had been admiral-of-the-fleet during the Crimean War (there was a drawing of his funeral at Balaclava in the *London Illustrated News* that used to be taken out reverently to show us on visits to our grandparents). Several women had been unusual too: on Mother's side there was an aunt who was a governess to the last of the Tsars; on Father's there was one who had been close to the Methodist preacher John Wellesley, and another who (unless I've imagined her) walked across Outer Mongolia.

Our parents' homes lay within a few miles of each other, in South London, at Blackheath and Burnt Ash Hill. Both had experienced poverty: Father had been a scholarship boy in a choir school in Malvern, and could remember a winter when he didn't have shoes (his father was branch manager of a very small bank);

Mother's father, who taught mathematics at Woolwich Military Academy, died at age forty-eight leaving nine children under the age of seventeen. Both parents were Labour-leaning, readers of Bernard Shaw and H. G. Wells. They were both hard workers – today they would be called 'workaholics' – both loved gardening and both were excellent drivers, but they didn't have what today are called 'qualifications'; and like others of their generation they weren't prepared for the post-World War One economy. Besides this, a streak of bad luck seems to have settled on the marriage from the beginning. This was concretised for me in a box full of blackened, twisted metal that sat in a shed at the bottom of Grandpa Boxer's garden. Mark and I used to rummage through it to drag out Father's cavalry sword, welded to its sheath. The other lumps were their wedding silver, all that was salvaged when their first home burnt down.

Not quite eighteen when World War One broke out, Father falsified his age to join up, emerging four years later a life-long pacifist with a medal and no training. He loved – in a very English, boyish, early-twentieth-century way – all machines, whatever their nature or purpose. One of his first gifts to me was a model of Stevenson's steam engine, one that actually made steam. After the war he took a quick course in civil engineering, which enabled him to add the initials AMICE to his name. But his love of 'tinkering' with machines, which became his way of earning a living, was really a form of play, and totally unaccompanied by a sense of salesmanship. He was an individualist craftsman, a maker-and-mender, intimidated by market trends and other car trade people. He told us they were all tricksters and thieves.

One of Father's favourite 'ploys' was laying out Mark's electric train set, which had tunnels and lights and double crossings and filled the whole sitting room. Mark mainly watched. Father also loved reading, passing on to me all his boyhood favourites: Jack London, Fenimore Cooper, Arthur Buchan. He was a shy, introverted man, a nail-biter and music-lover, who began towards the end of his life to write his autobiography for his grandchildren, under the title of *Diary of a Nobody*. Sadly he never finished it.

Mother was more complex. In spite of a Fabianism that veered at times towards a flighty kind of Communism, she clung to fragments (or figments) of her Edwardian childhood, and of a home where the children lived on the upper floor with two nannies and a housemaid, coming down after supper to recite poems to visitors, to be rewarded with a chocolate. From such occasions, and from bitter sibling rivalry, Mother had stored the maxim 'With lightning glance select the largest'. Residues of this grandeur had survived her father's death and passed down to us in her tastes and vetoes, as well as the stories she told us about her life before marriage. King George V had asked her questions about sun spots on a visit to Greenwich Observatory where she worked briefly. She had weekended in a few grand houses but also, as a Girl Guide leader and proto-feminist, had marched with Mrs Pankhurst for the vote. Orde Wingate had courted one of her younger sisters.

All this introduced an aristocratic undertone to her leftism. Right up to the end of World War Two she kept what we called her 'Wimbledon dress'. She always took her bath in the morning, did *The Times* crossword puzzle daily, and was fanatical about warming the supper plates. She enjoyed listening to the racing news and occasionally placed a small bet. I can't remember her minding anything we children did except making a noise when she was sleeping, or using vetoed words such as 'toilet', 'pardon' or 'serviette'. She suffered from insomnia and had her own special down pillow and cellulose blankets. She told funny, malicious stories about her sisters and brothers, and had a good stock of dirty limericks. Another of her guiding maxims, the one that best summarises her character, was 'Never apologise, never explain'.

When Father took us out for a treat, it was usually to a Lyon's Corner House; Mother preferred a pub lunch or a real restaurant with wine and napkins. Father was usually grubby from lying on his back under cars; he felt most at ease with his workers; he drank his morning tea out of an enormous cup he called his 'chamber pot'. Mother preferred coffee and served it black to visitors in elegant little demitasses.

The incompatibility at the core of most marriages emerged in our parents' case under economic pressure. The povery that dogged them wasn't the real poverty of the unemployed English working class or the Third World, it was a typically English middle-class poverty of anxiety and implicit 'standards', of a discrepancy between earning power and expectations. It wasn't that Father was 'hopeless' with money, or drank or ran after women. On the contrary, he had (alas) no extravagances, kept careful accounts, and was always puzzling over his narrow profit margins. Mother thought it should be easy to make money but wasn't serious about figures. Vague ambitions led her into home-based projects — dog-breeding, a herd of dairy goats, cane-chair mending, gardening for other people — that never quite realised their potential. Things would have worked out better if she had been an 'ordinary housewife'. Yet to say that is to deny her the right to her own character.

Mark inherited some things from both our parents: from Father his build and dark colouring (so pronounced he was often taken for an Indian), also his love of cricket and Englishness; from Mother a certain finesse and an ability to hold people's attention. But really Mark was self-made, emerging quite unpredictably from a very ordinary family background. There were other artists — one of Father's step-brothers, Noel, was a painter and engraver who died young of tuberculosis in Paris; our cousin Sandy Cunningham was a talented painter and printer. But for his sophistication, clothes' sense and wit there was no precedent at all. Not even an eccentric. His roots didn't support him.

Early childhood

I don't remember being jealous of Mark, yet why otherwise should I have been so struck by the importance of his three names (Charles Mark Edward) which reduced my solitary one to the marker of an unwanted girl? Or why should I have noticed the only half ironical way they referred to him as 'son and heir'? Yet he, first and most of all, brought out my maternal side. An early photo shows me clutching his rounded smocked figure with both arms, as if afraid he will fall. Aged perhaps one, he doesn't yet have his adorable grin.

It was while we were still at Sarratt, when Mark was four, that it was discovered that there was something wrong with his heart, a defect similar to the one believed to have caused the death of Mother's father. After that Mark lived under a special regime: he wasn't allowed to do boxing at school, while sports masters were instructed to take him off the field if his face started going grey. Mother worried about him continually, translating her worry into rules and restrictions. Much later, at home on holiday during World War Two, he had to bicycle five miles every day to get himself a bottle of special enriched milk. He was always very thin. It may be that his delicate health kept him close to home and Mother's orbit. He showed no interest in cars or engines or Father's workshop; they never did male things together such as going to football matches.

If he had fears about death he kept them to himself. He was a sunny, cheerful little boy, a smiler and a tease. As he grew up and took over his own life, Mother's special regime was gradually abandoned. He never adopted the habits of someone who has to be careful about his health.

At Sarratt, with Mother away all week, I tried to stand between Mark and the tyrannical 'Flinty', whose idea of children was to rub his nose in his pants whenever he had an 'accident' (this happened often and was the first sign that there was something wrong with his health). I hated Flinty passionately. She had carroty hair and warts on her face, and forced me to eat undercooked bacon fat. I never dared to complain to Mother, who thought Flinty was 'wonderful'.

If there was a school in the village it must have been judged unsuitable because it wasn't until I was nearly eight that I started attending school in Watford, the nearest town. Mother we only saw at weekends, Father only at breakfast, when he appeared grim and taciturn, immersed in financial cares. Mark was my little kingdom. Every day we were sent together on a 'five mile' walk while Flinty did the housework. We shared a playbox full of bricks and lead soldiers whose heads came off; we had our bath together, and together listened, terrified but fascinated, to Fu Man Chu on Radio Luxembourg. It was towards the end of the Sarratt period, when Mark was five or six, that he threw off my domination and made friends with the boy next door. Together they named me the enemy and, with drawing paper and pencils, riddled me with bullets. Each bullet *hurt*. It was only much later, remembering this incident, that I was struck by the fact that it was through drawing that Mark deposed me and liberated himself.

Another memory from this period is of playing Monopoly together. Mark always beat me in spite of the four years' difference in our ages, always managing to buy Park Lane and Mayfair while I landed up with Pentonville Road. I must have been a bad loser because he devised a system for evening out the odds, dealing me out a few good properties at the beginning. Probably it was a strategy for keeping me in the game but I've always been touched by it.

School eventually broke in on this rather isolated childhood. In spite of our money difficulties Mark was sent to private schools: first a day school in Watford, then a preparatory boarding school in Buckinghamshire (Boarsted?), later to Berkhamsted. He told me that the other boys talked mainly about the cars their fathers owned. This never happened at the day schools I went to. Mother used to confide in me her worries about his being bullied. Such is English family silence that we knew very little about his life at boarding school. But one of his letters to Father in India, written when he was maybe nine, asked 'Have you found a big friend yet?' Years later he told me that he developed story-telling as a way of beguiling bigger boys.

Boarsted boys wore bright pink caps. This is all I remember about Mark's prep school except for his descriptions of someone who taught there called Adrian Earle, who later turned up again as a louche London character. Already Mark must have had an eye for the kind of people who would inhabit his cartoons, the rich and would-be rich, people of a world in which no one in his family had ever set foot.

Later childhood and the war

A year or two before the war started Father's business picked up enough for us to leave Sarratt. We moved to a farmhouse at Leavesden, halfway between Watford and St Albans, set in undulating fields and woods. The house was thickly covered in ivy and had a big, stone-floored kitchen, and a cellar where Mother tried to grow mushrooms; there was also a 'secret' staircase and a conservatory with a passion-flower tree. It had a large, irregular garden full of trees and shrubberies that screened off the road. As a home it encouraged dreaminess and introspection. Away at school for most of the year, Mark was probably less attached to New House Farm than I was.

The war changed everything. Looking back from having lived through the war in Lebanon, I'm amazed how much more uprooted and dislocated we were by World War Two. It wasn't just the air-raids, the black-out and the rationing, it was the ending of familiar routines and contacts, a bleakness that penetrated every corner of our lives. Before the war, every Sunday regular as clockwork, we used to visit the grandparents in London: lunch with Grandpa and Grannie Boxer, tea with Grannie Jackson. With the war all such visits ended. For the whole six years we saw none of our relatives except Aunt Joan who came to stay because she had a war job at De Havillands. By the time the war was over the grandparents were dead, the aunts and uncles scattered and the cousins grown up.

Father's business suffered. Without enough capital to wait for better times he went back into the Army. In 1941 he was sent to India; there were no home leaves and we didn't see him again for four years. To eke out Father's Army pay Mother took 'PGs' (paying guests). Most of them helped with the washing up and became friends (those who didn't gradually noticed a chill and left). Our social life shifted, away from the pre-war friends with whom we had shared cheap summer cottages by the sea, towards the PGs and people close enough to reach by bicycle or walking. Mother made new friends in the local Fabian Society and Workers' Educational Association, who used to come out for Sunday tea and political discussions. Otherwise life was very dull. On Saturday mornings, Mother and I went in to Watford by bus to change library books. The cinema was out of the question unless it was a matinée, because the last bus to Leavesden left at 9 p.m. As a teenager I remember going to only one dance, at the local lunatic asylum. I think Mark was bored by this rural monotony. He never brought a friend home for the holiday. Probably he cared less than I did when New House Farm was scheduled for demolition, towards the end of the war, to make space for a large new council housing estate. Mother and I used to go out at night to pull out the surveyors' pegs.

In summer during the war Mark and I used to go to swim in the pool of our landlord, two or three miles away across the fields. It was a ten-by-twenty foot concrete pool with slimy green water, separated from the main house by a giant chestnut tree. No one ever came out to talk to us, we felt as if it was ours. At the shallow end stood side by side two small wooden changing huts. Time had eased out knots from their creosote planks, leaving eyeholes which Mark used to peep through whenever I had school friends to stay. He also loved to dance naked around the huts, whooping and yelling. He was so thin that he could never manage to float, swimming submerged under inches of greenish water until forced to come up to breathe.

There's no doubt he was coming out an entertainer though Mother and I didn't realise it then. The word Mother used a lot of him in those days was 'clowning': 'Mark's such a clown!' I can visualise him, face screwed up, thumbs held to ears, fingers held out and wiggling in mockery. Mother also used to call him 'bats ears'. I was surprised when one of the PGs remarked on his 'lovely dark eyes'. Up to then I'd thought of him as just a skinny brat.

In 1943, despairing of a quick end to the war, Mother sold Father's garage equipment (stored in the conservatory) and bought a herd of pedigree dairy goats. These were in addition to the other animals we had: hens, ducks, four dogs and a cat. Looking after all this livestock as well as the PGs wore Mother out. She tramped around with buckets from dawn to dusk, no longer bothering to change out of dungarees. Mark and I shared a hatred of the goats. They had malevolent yellow eyes and required immense quantities of fresh branches twice daily in order to produce milk that smelt slightly of vomit. We could never go away because of their iron feeding and milking schedule. Mother's socialist principles also obstructed her money-making motives, making it impossible for her to charge a proper price for the milk.

Whereas I oscillated moodily between attachment and rebellion towards

Mother, Mark early evolved towards a kind of affectionate detachment. This difference between us became clear to me the day Mother tried to spank him with a slipper for refusing to carry out some domestic chore. He must have been twelve or thirteen. He slipped out of her reach, and – this was the revelation for me – turned to grin at her mockingly. It was like the overturning of an icon.

During the holidays we used to spend hours guiltily lounging in the drawing room playing cards or listening to Mother's gramophone records on an old hand-wound His Master's Voice. She had all of Hutch, and Cicely Courtneidge singing 'Doing What Comes Naturally'. Compared with our parents, Mark and I were sub-urban decadent. Instead of Wells and Priestley we read Oscar Wilde and Evelyn Waugh. We made our own lino-cut Christmas cards and when *Picture Post* started coming out we cut out the 'Modern Masters' to stick on our bedroom walls. Yet there was an ambivalence in our alliance. I felt guilty because I should have been out digging the garden or helping with the goats; but Mother didn't like arguments about the way she did things, and I needed an escape from her regime. Mark was less influenced by her, but more sensitive to her moods; he didn't like it to look as if we were being conspiratorial.

Father came back from the war soon after it ended and there began a long-drawn out period of crisis that ended in 1949 with our parents' separation. Used to running things herself, Mother took Father's return badly. She felt that he had had a 'lovely war' waited on by batmen, whereas she had broken herself looking after home and children. Father went over the goats' milk accounts and found that they were making a loss. He also found out about the sale of his equipment. Politically Mother had moved to the left: Father's mild Labour views now struck her as positively Tory. Their arguments were embittered by the usual money problems. The approaching demolition of New House Farm added to the atmosphere of desperation. Mother threatened suicide.

It was around this time that Mark and I were sitting alone together in the kitchen. Suddenly he said, apropos of nothing, 'I have to get out of here.' It must have marked a critical turning point, a rupture with childhood. Was it that summer or the next that he covered the kitchen walls with cartoons, as far as I knew his first? I connect these two events as revealing a decision and a talent that up to then I hadn't noticed. Mired in our parents' warfare I never imagined escape was possible, nor that life could be different. Perhaps this was the moment when the Mark everyone would know was born, almost by parthenogenesis?

Mother was worried about Mark's future, fearing he wouldn't get to university, a goal she set great store by. He was weak in Latin, essential then for getting into Cambridge. She even approached her brother who was 'in the City' to see if Mark could be taken into the firm. I don't know if Mark's school record was really so weak or whether she was fussing. He wasn't good at the conventional subjects but a teacher who noticed him reading *War and Peace* had taken an interest in him; by the time he reached the sixth form he was in good standing.

At sixteen Mark was tall, lanky, tousle-headed. There's a photo of us standing together in Nyon (Switzerland) and he already overtops me. It was the summer of 1947, our first trip abroad; we were staying with Father's Swiss cousins. For much of the time there I was in shock after receiving a twelve-page letter from the current boyfriend saying he didn't think we should see each other any more. Mark was very sweet and sympathetic. I guessed he must have been having experiences of his own because he told me that all the girls at Berkhamsted Girls' School were tarts. On the night train from Paris to Geneva he got chatting with a girl in the next seat and I saw that they were holding hands.

Mother's fears were resolved in 1948/9, Mark's final year at Berkhamsted. This was the year when he 'came out', acting so brilliantly in the lead role of Shaw's *St Joan* that Shepherd, the Provost of King's College, who happened to be in the audience, practically offered him a place on the spot. He told Mother not to worry about Mark's Latin. Mother wrote to me about this exciting episode, which I missed. By this time I had left university and was in Milan teaching English to the children of an Italian industrialist.

Divergence

What are the distortions I ask myself and, even more, what are the gaps in my memories of Mark? The memories I have (perhaps memories of memories?) seem to focus on moments when I realised how unalike we were; or, alternatively, moments of closeness and alliance. But there are stretches of emptiness, areas of ignorance, everyday things forgotten, questions never asked. Did I never ask him what it felt like to be a not-too-strong nine-year-old in an English boys' boarding school? How account for the fact that someone so sociable never talked about friends at school and never brought anyone home to visit? After adolescence our lives diverged so much that I never discovered what the episodes I remembered meant to him. Anyway he didn't enjoy cosy chats about the past.

In the autumn of 1949, Mark's first term at Cambridge, our parents finally split up. I was back from Italy by now and wanted to live in London. Since both of us were jobless, Mother and I shacked up together in a basement off Sloane Square. The basement was rent-free in return for Mother cleaning the stairs and putting out the milk bottles. I started a Pitman's typing course in Holborn and worked afternoons for a historian in Maida Vale. We were almost destitute. I remember an old friend buying me a Wetherall skirt for job interviews. Later I got a job as copy-writer with an advertising agency on a salary of about £8 a week. Father moved into a one-room flat opposite his workshop, and eventually married the widow next door.

I visited Mark in his first term at Cambridge and found him already doing cartoons for *Granta*. Somebody famous, I've forgotten who, dropped into his rooms while I was there, and there were other elegant, witty friends. A total provincial, I was stunned by these signs of success, happy for him but also a bit intimidated.

The atmosphere of Cambridge was quite different from post-war Oxford, livelier and more fun-loving. However I only visited Mark there once again, for a goodbye party, after deciding to give up advertising and take a job teaching English in a women's college in Baghdad. Because of this absence I missed the famous *Granta* scandal, when Mark was sent down for having published a poem by Anthony de Hoghton that the proctors judged blasphemous. It was only a few weeks before finals and Mother wrote me an agonised letter, fearing that his career was ruined.

At the end of my first year in Baghdad (where British teachers earned £100 a month, more than Iraqi heads of colleges) Mark and I spent a month together near Palermo – I still have a sketch book we shared – but from then on we met only occasionally. Of that period I still hold memories of his extraordinary charm quite unlike that of anyone I have ever met, spontaneous and kind – 'nice' was a key word then. He seemed really to focus on anyone, however dull, whom he happened to be with. He was also exhibitionistic (I remember his embarrassing, braying laugh once at a London theatre), and funny and witty. From those days, or perhaps Cambridge, comes his inversion of Connolly's fat man/thin man epigram: 'Outside every thin man there's a fat man trying to get in.' In spite of his charm he was totally professional about work and could be brusque if telephoned at the office.

Our childhood alliance survived separation at first. In 1953 I married Yusif Sayigh and settled permanently in Beirut; in 1956 he married Arabella Stuart. They generously lent us their home in Chelsea in the summer of 1959 when we were on our way to a sabbatical in the United States. Mark continued to encourage me to write, inviting me to contribute to *Granta* and later to the *Sunday Times* colour section, sending me things he'd written (his real ambition, he once told me, was to write a novel). Gradually, however, our lives diverged, the geographical distance perhaps only delaying the surfacing of a deeper divergence, one not easily bridged by letters, gifts or visits. Mark wasn't drawn to the Middle East, perhaps was disappointed that I didn't 'make more' of my connection with it. His letters, once so warm and affectionate, gradually became shorter and drier, sometimes signed by secretaries. When I passed through London, it seemed each time that the time he could spare for a meeting was less, his greeting cooler. He wasn't interested in my world and I lacked the language to ask about his (questions are in any case a sign of dissociation). After a while there seemed to be only one thing left to talk about – Mother.

In the late sixties, at one of these brief meetings, I asked him for news of a friend, someone we both knew. Mark said he hadn't seen him lately and added, 'I can't stand *ordinary* people.' I've always hated dichotomies and I suppose it was then that, for me, the sibling cord snapped.

THE GRANTA STAFF WELCOMING THE SUMMER

Richard Wollheim

I met Mark in the mid-1950s. Memory suggests to me that I first set eyes on him as he stepped out of a litter, dressed only in a leopard's skin, a wreath of oak leaves in his hair, at the Roman Ball organised by the Royal College of Art. He was of medium height, thin, with dark, curly hair, cut unfamiliarly short. As his feet touched the ground, he gave a quick, nervous smile. This image does much justice to Mark's spectacular arrival over my horizon, but memory plays me false in that I am pretty sure I had met him earlier than this, though not by much. It was certainly just after he had been sent down from Cambridge – sent down, or rusticated, or possibly gone down but under some pressure – for having published in a literary magazine he edited a poem found objectionable by the university authorities. I mention this incident not only because it dates our meeting better, it seems, than recollection unaided, but because it also reveals a link that Mark and I had before we ever met. I don't think that after we met we ever referred to it. Mark was a man very easily embarrassed – so perhaps am I – which may be, may not be, the reason why we never raised the subject. But it seemed to me of interest at the time, it continued to do so, and more recently it has intrigued me. I start with it, and I hope that the rather lengthy detour justifies itself.

I went back to Oxford immediately after the war, and, during the three years that, on and off, I spent there, I became very friendly with a rather over-lifesize and altogether remarkable character called Anthony de Hoghton. Anthony at this stage was a postgraduate student, in itself something of an oddity in Oxford and in Anthony's case completely unexplained. He was a man of prodigious gifts, subject to abrupt and wild changes of mood: he could switch in a flash from exuberant joviality to morose cantankerousness. His appearance was striking. He was more or less an albino, with pale, thinning hair, corpulent, and with heavy, Hanoverian features and the complexion of a small baby.

He avoided dressing like the conventional upper-class young man: he wore oddly assorted tweeds, and he sought out the flashiest ties he could find at Charvet or Turnbull and Asser. 'Do you admire this tie?' he would say provocatively, picking it up from his stomach and staring at it. He was never less than freshly scented, and, when he went in for one of his bouts of not washing and not shaving, which became increasingly frequent, he drenched himself in eau-de-cologne. Somewhat incongruously he walked with one of those fat-boy walks, and, as he propelled himself along the High, brushing his thighs with his hands, his head held up as if he was sniffing the air, people turned and stared after him, and this indeed was how I first became aware of him. It was about two or three weeks later that, going to call on Phyllis Young one evening after dinner, I saw, as the door was opened, stretched out in a large white armchair, his forehead glistening with sweat, this great spectacle of Oxford. For a moment he turned on me his hooded, colourless eyes: then he turned back, as though he had already wasted too much time. 'Go on Phyllis,' he said. 'Go on with the story.' And he ground his teeth together. There was a whole side to Anthony, often suppressed, which continuously played an irritable, verminous old man. What I most learnt about Anthony that evening was the vast range of emotion that his face could assume. It could express total incredulity, when his pale eyebrows would rise up into two semicircles until they seemed to touch his receding hairline. It could, only too easily, express total indignation, and then his lips stuck out into an enormous pout into which his chin vanished and he hummed with rage. Most disconcerting of all was when in a second his face crumpled up like a handkerchief and he shook with a high-pitched giggle.

Anthony could be a very funny man, and it was this and a real, if somewhat strangulated, warmth of character, and not just his outrageousness, though that certainly played some part, that won him friends and in some cases brought people totally under his sway. I think that he had some kind of need to exercise authority. Anthony came from an old Catholic family, whose religion he had long abandoned. Son of the senior baronet of the United Kingdom, he had survived an unhappy childhood. He seldom referred to it, and one story, which he told often, must have stood in for many. His mother had just died, and Anthony, who was still a schoolboy, was looking in the local newspaper when he read, to his complete surprise, that Sir Cuthbert had asked one of his 'milkmaids' – it was the word that Anthony always used – to marry him. Anthony combined an Almanach de Gotha kind of snobbery with a restless hatred of the established order. There was a deep destructive intensity to Anthony, and this ultimately singed his whole character, gifts and all.

Anthony was a poet, and, by the time I met him, he had published a thin volume of verse in the manner of Laforgue. He was something of a scholar, certainly a pedant, of the French language, and had a magpie knowledge of late medieval, Renaissance, and baroque literature. He cultivated the acquaintance of a small group of elderly, reclusive men of letters, who had squandered their gifts in solitary drunkenness, or in the pursuit of boys, or in avarice. These were not Anthony's ways, but he had an affinity with them. He was certainly a heavy, if fastidious, drinker – he liked to drink buckets of good burgundy – but he was not, at least at this stage, a lone drinker. Anthony's tastes were for women, and he talked of a particular friend he had in London, a relation of Leonard Woolf, but he seemed to have a preference for women who brought out the worst in him. At times, it is true, Anthony could be avaricious, but more often he was ominously generous. As a meal came to an end and the bill approached – and, if it was a waiter who knew Anthony, he could often be observed putting in an extra loop round a table or two, to delay his arrival — a series of emotions, far in excess of the situation, passed across Anthony's face. But there were times when he entertained with the abandon of the Count of Monte Cristo.

In early January 1947, I arrived in Florence in response to a summons from Anthony. It was my first time in Florence, my first time in Italy. Having taken Schools, I had been staying in Paris briefly, then with a cousin of my father's in Zurich. The cousin, who was called Hans Feist, was a middle-aged aesthete, and he passed his day either trying to sell the remnants of his mother's collection of Renaissance objects or engaged in long sentimental telephone conversations with Austrian or Hungarian ladies of title. When I received a telegram from Anthony, I had virtually no money, and the very few pounds I had Hans persuaded me I needed to have smuggled out of Switzerland. He arranged for a chiropodist to meet me on the train, collect my money, and deliver Italian lire to me in Como, at the house of two extremely old ladies, the granddaughters or great-granddaughters of Manzoni, who lived in what was in effect a shrine to the great writer. They kindly asked me to stay the night, and we talked in whispered French. By the time I arrived in Florence snow had fallen. Anthony, who seemed delighted to see me, had taken for us a suite that ran the length of the Albergo Minerva and looked out on to the façade of Santa Maria Novella. It was completely unheated. My recollection is that we had an amusing enough time, though for me the excitement associated with being in a new city, a new country, never materialised. It was too like being back in the George at Oxford and the question was would Anthony, would he not, insult the waiter. After a very few days I had to leave and something I must have unguardedly said led Anthony to abandon the plans for further travel that he certainly had had and to decide to come back with me to Geneva where my cousin normally lived and indeed to move into the small *rive-gauche* hotel where I was going to stay with him. There was nothing I could do to stop what followed. Anthony had decided that he and Hans would get on badly, and they did. Anthony got flu. When he had recovered, by which time I was back in England, he asked Hans for a letter of introduction to Cocteau. Hans agreed. It was only as Anthony was climbing the old worn staircase of the Palais Royale that he thought of looking inside the envelope, which had been left unsealed, and there he read his name: 'Monsieur Anthony de Hoghton, *la machine infernale*'.

As time passed, Anthony's extravagance, his bizarre destructiveness, his isolation from the world of others, except for an ever refined sense of how he could cause offence, grew more florid. He bought a large Mercedes, which was said to have belonged to the German General Staff, and, the first time out, he crashed it in a head-on collision on a long, straight section of the Roman road to Bath. He became great friends with the Dylan Thomases, and I remember a party which ended with Anthony taking Caitlin off to bed while an overturned candle gradually burnt its way through the floorboard; the floorboard was never mended. Briefly

Anthony stayed in London with a great friend of mine, Benedict Nicolson, and one evening Harold came to dinner, which was an important event in Ben's life. Anthony offered to cook, which he could do very well. Dinner was excellent until Anthony produced a dessert, which he insisted on everyone trying: it was a large bowl of tinned guavas with anchovies. And Anthony could still be funny. One day, hearing that I had flu, he called on me in London. He sat on the edge of the bed in his overcoat and started to recount a story of Arabian Nights complexity – story within a story – and then he paused. 'Am I boring you?' he asked. 'No,' I said. 'In which case,' he said, 'I shan't go on.' It was the old Anthony. But now he didn't laugh: he glowered.

Getting Mark sent down was for Anthony the repetition of an earlier triumph. His first victim, at Oxford, was an old friend, a companion in many escapades. Having got the friend to invite him to dine in Christ Church, Anthony waited until the end of dinner, then he emptied his silver tankard with a flourish, he held the tankard under the table, pissed into it, and deliberately placed it on the table. A scout, who was serving in Hall, and to whom Anthony, it transpired, was a familiar figure, noticed the tankard, took it up to the High Table, handed it round, and asked first the Dean, then the dons and their guests to identify the steaming contents. The outcome was sealed. Some time after this Anthony moved to Cambridge, and he carried with him a ballad of the sort into which, by this time, all his poetic talents were channelled: scabrous, rich in anecdote, and driven by fierce comic energy. When I was still at Oxford, I had introduced Anthony to an old school friend of mine, later a great scholar, whose mother was famous among us for her political views: she is supposed to have said that she liked being in Italy because there the poor had to beg for their living. Anthony got himself invited to tea with her, drew her out, and it was to catch her tone and idiom that he was inspired to write what was the first of these new ballads. Anthony then went to my friend, told him of the existence of the poem, and said that, since it was likely that he would be reading it to a number of other people, it was only polite, indeed courtesy demanded, that he, my friend, should be the first to hear it. Anthony then recited the poem with bardic grandeur. The ballad that Anthony took with him to Cambridge was about God. The first line went, 'God is in his garage, cranking up his Bentley'. I would not have thought that there was much in the poem that could have been seriously objected to, even by the standards of then, not just of now. But Anthony, as things turned out, knew better. He submitted his ballad to *Granta* when Mark was out of Cambridge, it was printed, and what happened next is the very point at which my story began.

Once I got to know Mark, the question that intrigued me was how had Mark and Anthony become friends. After all, to like Anthony when Mark must have begun to know him, by which time he was already sly, vindictive, treacherous, *la machine infernale*, was a quite different matter from liking him when we became friends, when he was, by and large, open, and capable of wonderful generosity and high spirits. Then he was a difficult man, now he was dangerous. Nor did the two seem to me to have much in common. Mark in those days was dazzlingly elegant, and in a quite new way, utterly unlike the permanently exhausted dandies I knew from Oxford. He might have been one of those young men whom at that period bewildered English travellers started to take note of, bustling through the galleries of Milan or along the arcaded streets of Bologna, catching an occasional glimpse of themselves in some reflecting surface. He was quick, eager, ambitious, with a marvellous sweetness of manner. There was no obvious reason why Anthony's upper-class decrepitude should have appealed to him. Then, as I gradually got to know Mark better, I found the answer to my question. What I learnt taught me something that was exclusively about him. What Mark preserved was a capacity to observe people, to observe and to respond to them, in a way that lay outside the conventions of moral or polite society. He could put aside all conceptions of what they would, or should, or might become, and look to them simply as they were in themselves, no matter what they ever made of it. He looked to them for some little inner flame, some little inner bird, that lurked within them and made them different, even if, should it actually work its way to the surface, the cost would be terrible. It is the same blind faith in innerness, in the marvellousness of oddity, that Proust showed us in Marcel in his continuing fascination with Charlus, long after the utter impossibility of his character has become manifest, indeed even as he heaps upon the younger man completely senseless abuse. It is the child's view of life, for it is like liking the grown-ups for the wonderful stories they have it in them to tell, or for the faces they can pull, or for the strange upsets they can bring about in the most ordinary, humdrum, summer's day. And Mark was something of a child. Though he led a full life, busy with incident and not untouched by tragedy, he also gave the impression that he hadn't really started on it. He was still on the outside, he was still looking in, and, as to putting his foot over the threshold, for much of the time he suggested that he would rather not. Like many men who retain this childishness, Mark was inconsolable.

Unlike most men whom we think of as still in some part children, Mark had, at any rate from the time I first knew him, a very decided idea about what he wanted to do: that is, he had a decided idea about what he wanted to bring about, but how to do it, what field he should be in, what job he should go for, was always something left open. One result was that I never knew precisely what job Mark did have. I knew, for instance, that he worked on a glossy magazine, but I didn't know which one. I knew that he worked on a Sunday newspaper, but I didn't know which one. I knew that he worked for a publisher, but I was uncertain for whom. Of course, I didn't care, and, if I had, Mark would have told me: nor am I suggesting that Mark lacked conscientiousness. It just was that he was more interested in the ends that he saw himself as trying to realise.

One incident I think of in particular as evincing the freedom of spirit that Mark preserved so well. One of the last brainchildren of Hugh Gaitskell's was a Labour

Party Commission on Advertising, set up just before he died. Hugh asked me to be on it, and I agreed. The commission had broad terms of reference and it was intended to probe deep into the effects of advertising on the economy, on society, and on the distribution of information. It bore all the hallmarks of Hugh's thinking for better and for worse. The breadth of reference was Hugh's idea, and characteristically, it was bitterly resented, indeed the very existence of the commission was bitterly resented, by his successor as leader. However, it also came second nature to Hugh to think that all men of goodwill would, in politics as elsewhere, converge on the truth, except in one circumstance: for it is imperative that they are well informed. Accordingly, in setting up the commission, Hugh insisted that it should have on it three overt representatives of advertising. Then Hugh gave us as chairman a remarkable man, who combined total determination, naïve high-mindedness, and political acumen in proportions familiar to me from the Master of my old Oxford college: our chairman was the ageing Lord Reith, founder of the BBC, who in a famous television interview had recently complained that he had never been 'stretched'. Here, in the very composition of the commission, were laid the conditions of complete deadlock, which was made worse by the increasing hostility of Transport House, which removed our secretarial assistance, and by the revelation that at least half of the members of the commission who were not supposed to have anything to do with advertising were in its pay. I can recall the all but total frustration of long meetings, at first monthly, then fortnightly, then weekly, then twice-weekly, in ill-lit committee rooms, the attendance sparse, and always the relentless bonhomie of the advertisers who never missed a session. Occasionally Lord Reith erupted in anger. 'What does it feel like,' he said to the head of a famous advertising agency, 'what does it feel like, I wonder, to be a man like you?'

One subject on which we were making some progress was the effect of advertising on newspapers. The advertisers attempted to assure us that the effect was completely benign: it was a purely financial link, there was no question of undue influence, and, if any advertiser tried it on, it would be sure to be – though why was not explained to us – 'self-defeating'. Anyone on a newspaper, they said, would confirm this. At this stage I thought of Mark. The somewhat menacing tone of the advertisers convinced me that it would be quite wrong even to suggest to Mark that he should appear before the whole commission. But, Lord Reith put it to me, was it possible that my friend would agree to lunching with the two of us, when he might talk freely, and then Lord Reith would vouch for what he had been told. There remained a risk. I put the idea to Mark, who without a moment's hesitation said he would love to do it. We lunched in the House of Lords, and Mark was wonderfully lucid. He explained exactly how it was that the advertising manager of a large newspaper anticipated the demands of the advertisers and how the advertisers were confident that he would do so, so there was no need for anything improper to be said. Then he gave as an example how since travel advertising, and in particular the advertisements of the airlines, had increased and the colour supplements had become dependent on this subsidy, the statistics of aircrashes had been given less and less prominence. Lord Reith, who was a tremendous innocent in all matters of which he didn't have first-hand experience, listened with his enormous mouth wide open.

The confrontation of the two men was something to watch. Both were, in their immensely different ways, wizards of charm, and there is no reason to think that either of them was less self-conscious than the other on this score. Lord Reith was something of a giant, who at this period looked exactly like the film actor, Alastair Sim. He breathed heavily, and, as he stood in front of Mark, he gave the impression that with a big huff he could have blown him away. Mark was slender and looked as youthful as he did when I saw him step out of the Roman litter. As lunch progressed, the two men got on very well, and, when Mark had to leave, a slightly filmy look came over Lord Reith's eyes as happened, I was beginning to notice, whenever he met anyone who was young and manifestly gifted. I got the feeling that, forty years earlier, in the days of Savoy Hill, Lord Reith would have given Mark a job on the spot, had he been able to satisfy himself on the subject of Mark's sexual morals. On Mark's side, I could see that he was captivated by something untamed, unstretched in this great, craggy ogre of a man, the unreconstructed son of the manse. He winced at the hard, bony handshake Lord Reith gave him, and he covered it with a bright smile. 'The other day,' Lord Reith announced to the commission at our next meeting, looking sprightlier than he had for some time, 'Professor Wollheim and I had an *exceptionally* interesting lunch,' and he reported with great care exactly what Mark had said. The advertisers, with all due respect, counselled caution. 'Just one informant,' they said. 'And anonymous,' they added. From the way they looked at one another it was clear that they would have loved to have known his identity. What Mark had done had been, I could see, a courageous act. Indeed I was often to feel — and not only in this context — that, had Mark been a few years older, he would probably have been a war-hero.

Mark believed that any institution, certainly any for which he worked, should be judged by the standards of what it could become, or what it ought to be like. It was this belief, and not just friendship for me, not just the prospect of meeting one of the oddest figures in British life, that led him to lunch with Lord Reith. Had Mark's employer charged him with being disloyal, as, I suppose, he might have done, for accepting the invitation, Mark, I am sure, would have been above caring. He thought of loyalty differently: it was loyalty to some ideal that gripped him. But also it was, as I have suggested, that any job that Mark took on was for him invariably part of something bigger.

What was it then that Mark really wanted to do? What did he want to achieve? What was this end to which he thought of the various jobs he accepted as means? It was not always easy for an outsider to know. Mark was a veiled character. But this does not reflect upon his own resolve. Mark, as I see him over the years, wanted to change things, to alter taste, to give people clear standards, to arouse the world around him a little: he wanted to make books and photographs and women's hair and museums and coffee pots and the foyers of offices and the food on the table look different, and to do all this in the interest of modernity. The modern look would be clean, witty, and adapted to emancipated life in a great city. His early models, both of which were lost on me, were Fornasetti and the *New Yorker*. They were the front-runners of contemporary Italy and yesterday's America.

I remember Mark telling me that, surprisingly, he could never learn a foreign language, and consequently travel in Italy, travel in Europe, disappointed him. But I remember vividly Mark's arrival in the United States. It was late November 1959. We were in New York. Mark had come alone, and he rang us up. We had made an arrangement for that evening, and we were going with the boyfriend of a famous modernist architect and a young princess he had in tow to the Harlem Drag Ball: would he like to come with us? Mark had only just got off the plane. He was weighed down with fatigue. He said, as we anticipated, Yes. The Harlem Drag Ball is – 'is', or perhaps 'was', for I have no idea whether it still goes on – not a ball, but it was in Harlem, and it was the apotheosis of drag. It would have stretched the imagination of Toulouse-Lautrec. On what was in those days the only night in the year when a man was permitted by the law to appear on the streets of New York in women's clothes – the night of Thanksgiving Day, which ended on the stroke of midnight – a sloping plank was set up to run half the length of the vast, faded Lennox Ballroom, and for about two hours a slow-moving stream of drag queans climbed a short step-ladder and then processed down the gangway, exhibiting their charms in keeping with the roles they assumed. From time to time there was a slight scuffle at the head of the gangway. Someone would pause for an ovation longer than those behind thought right. They pushed and shoved, and the procession resumed. The cast of characters was phantasmagoric. Some paraded singly, some moved slowly forward in tableaux: Mae West, Jeannette Macdonald, Madame du Barry, a group of Weimar lesbians waving long black cigarette holders, Little Red Riding Hood, a tiny Southern bride and her black lady's maid, Shirley Temple, Miss Whiplash, the Queen of Sheba, the Statue of Liberty. Mark's eyes shut with exhaustion, then abruptly they clicked open again. A seraphic smile settled on his face. All around him little inner flames, little inner birds, were scratching their way out. Then at a quarter to midnight a giant scream went up, and great burly men and weedy pock-marked boys and many, many others were out in the streets, shouting for cabs, struggling out of their ball-dresses, dashing for home before the police were licensed to crack open their heads. Reality was descending, and Mark could no longer keep his eyes open a moment longer. We dropped him off at his hotel for his first night's sleep in New York.

In the mid-1960s, when my life was somewhat in limbo, Arabella and Mark were the most unquestioning, the most loyal of friends. I saw them frequently. Meanwhile Mark and I continued a habit which had developed earlier and was of a sort very rare in my life: we had lunch together regularly. We had started in the fifties in the new Sloane Street bistros, then we moved to kebab houses and then to the better Tandoori restaurants in the neighbourhood of Euston. They were intimate occasions, and intimacy meant for Mark that they would usually begin with his rather nervously raising some big issue that was on his mind. It might be censorship, or socialism, to which he retained an allegiance, or the upbringing of children, or visiting friends in hospital, or what an intellectual was, or what it was to be corrupted by the world. In the course of serious conversation intensity often led Mark to reverse syllables or to bring words out in the wrong order. Then he fumbled for poise. In later years he occasionally brought with him a girl whom he currently looked to for hope. Once he started to tell me how the drawings that he was now doing with increasing assurance gave him a form of satisfaction he no longer anticipated. He spoke about it hesitantly as though he didn't want to spoil the pleasure. But from the way he talked it was clear that this was something that brought together for him old interests of his which he had despaired of uniting: succinctness, visual wit, the challenge of an activity that couldn't be completed at all unless it was done to perfection, an appeal that transcended social barriers, a record, a history perhaps, of the ephemeral. Mark would not have described it like that himself. He would have gone to great lengths not to describe it like that. He treated himself with irony, and sometimes the irony came close to ridicule: he was, I believe, a man who lived much of his life in fear of being laughed at.

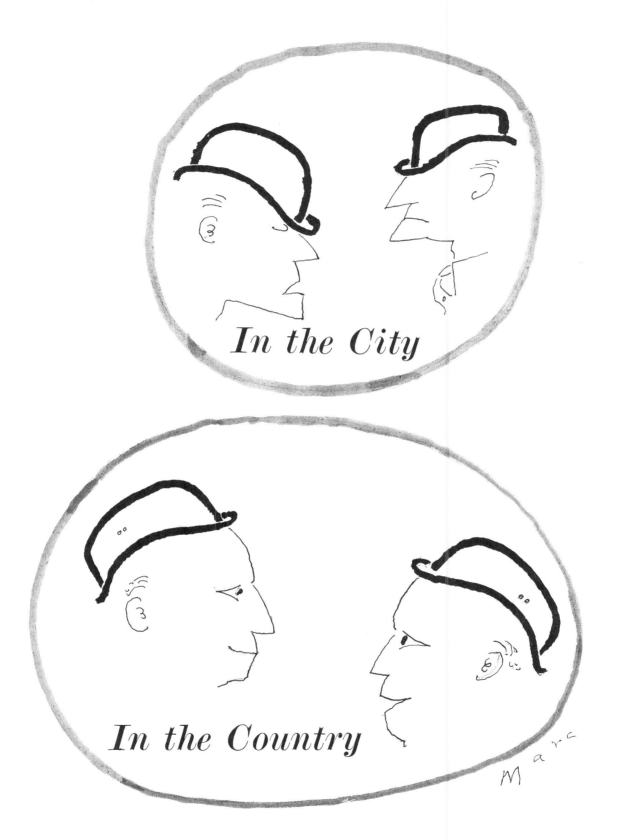

Peter Eyre

'I often have the same dream,' Mark told me. He was living alone in an apartment after his marriage to Arabella had come sadly to an end. 'I'm in a sort of helicopter – or maybe I am the helicopter – and I'm hovering over a party where I can see a lot of friends. But I can't land. I can't get to the party. It's really a nightmare.' Mark let out his explosive guffaw, a short falsetto shriek. But it was obvious he was not all that amused.

I had got to know Mark quite well, having met him first with Francis Wyndham in the early sixties, but I think I was probably more a friend of Arabella's than Mark's. I was a regular visitor at their house, a frequent dinner guest, and knew them very much as a couple. In 1974 they kindly allowed me to borrow their house for a ball – and I am sure I then went up a little in Mark's estimation, because he enjoyed, even loved, social events, almost any social event fascinated him. He took great pleasure in all the little dramas attached to this party – who was coming, who wasn't invited, who was definitely coming although definitely not invited, and the day after the party, which of my semi-criminal friends had stolen all the silver (hired silver, fortunately). I think this single social event gave him a false impression of my sociability, for when he found himself alone in his bachelor quarters some years later, and I was living conveniently near, he would call and arrange to meet me for dinner, not perhaps the dazzling entertainments he would have preferred, but rather low-key meals *à deux*. It was then we really became friends. The fact was he hated being on his own. I think he hated being alone more than anyone I have ever known. I actually liked being on my own, it certainly did not worry me. That seemed to become the leitmotiv of our dialogue.

Mark wanted activity all the time, and when he hit a low point in his life, he became desperate and attempted suicide. The solitary life was unbearable. I remember Mark, still full of pills and stumbling over words, somehow managing to describe the absurdity of this incident. 'That psychiatrist came round, just after I woke up. I couldn't believe it. He asked me what I dreamed. Really.' Another guffaw. This truly nightmarish episode had already become for him something inherently farcical. I visited him frequently during that period, and always left confident he would soon recover, and move on.

I think of Mark as someone who probably suffered a lot, but refused tragedy, and chose a more tolerable view of the world. I think that was in his work, caricatures which inspired affection but could be devastatingly critical.

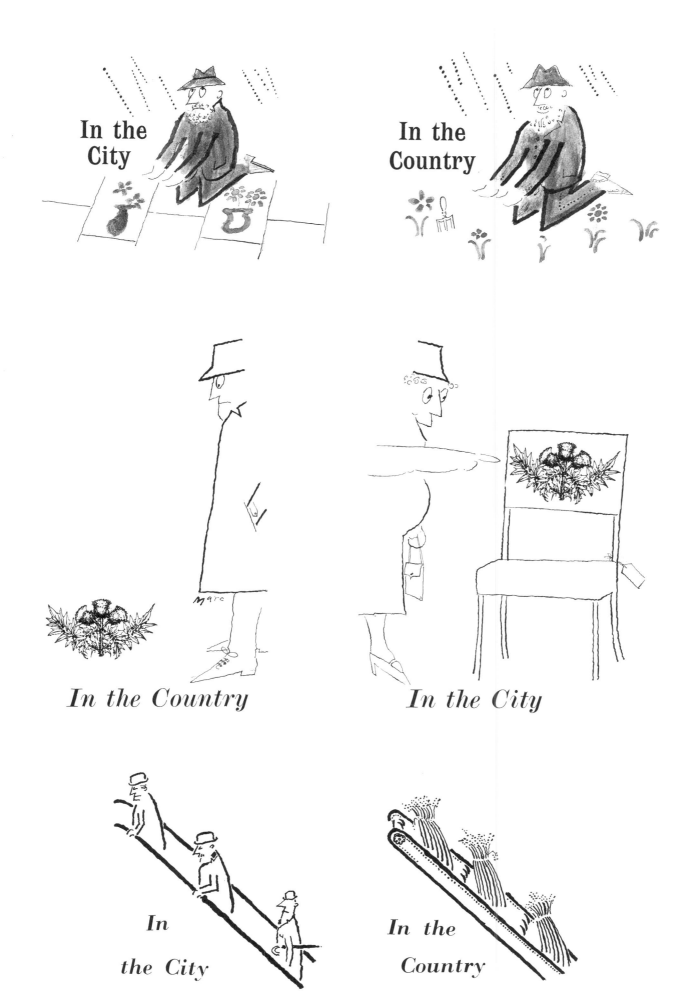

In the
City

In the
Country

In the Country

In the City

In

the City

In the

Country

Once staying with him and Arabella in the country, he said to me: 'You're very hard to draw. Those portraits of you by Cecil are ridiculous.' Beaton had done two drawings of me, very romantic sketches, which had been published along with a profile of me in *Vogue*. I was quite flattered by the spread. 'One day I might try,' he said threateningly. He picked up his pad, and we talked away, while he doodled. 'It's not very good, but it's sort of all right,' he said handing me a piece of paper. On it was a very economical drawing of a bald, dull-eyed, defeated man with puffy cheeks and an undefined mouth. I was horrified. 'Thanks,' I said after a long pause. 'Well, it's much more like you than that crap by Cecil.' Another guffaw.

I don't think of Mark as cruel. On the contrary, I think of him as someone very sweet, thoughtful and tender with his friends. I liked his individual way of pronouncing words, delicate and precise. He had a beautiful smile, charm, grace. As I think of him now I see him in motion – talking, turning his head suddenly away in another direction, whispering, leaning intently towards someone, flirting, moving like a dancer, and in the drawing room sometimes like a stage lounge lizard, playing cricket with real flair, running, laughing, drawing, writing, dashing to the telephone, dancing with real flair, darting this way and that.

Yet the happiest I ever saw him was not long before he died, lying very still in his garden one sunny afternoon, watching his girls playing, and smiling adoringly at Anna, his voice now very light and feeble. 'She's wonderful,' he said. There was no guffaw.

Joanna, I think you ought to go and investigate. Someone is making a great deal of noise downstairs.

Don't worry, it's probably the au pair registering her annoyance at the lack of food in the refrigerator.

Simon, something rather flattering has happened: we've been burgled.

But they haven't taken anything of real value. Our collection of thirties objects is untouched.

It's really rather depressing; it shows so convincingly the complete lack of taste of the lower class.

Have you seen this scheme to route the Stansted extension slap through NW1 ?

What a marvellous opportunity for a really valid protest movement. Moira can do a TV programme; we can have a party; and the Touch-Paceys can design a protest button.

I'm just going up to your den to draft a letter to the Times. We'll have some genuinely distinguished signatures for a change. In fact it's my great opportunity to be listed under the magical cross-heading 'from Professor Ayer and others'.

Congratulations! I've just heard at the residents' committee that the developers are going to make you a huge offer for your house. They need it for a petrol station.

Perhaps we've been rather hasty. I was beginning to feel dubious about aligning ourselves with the Betjemanites against the irresistible force of an immovable trend.

David Sylvester

Our professional colleagues tend to inspire affection in us when they don't inspire hatred or contempt. We feel a warmth towards those with whom we work well, and they are likely to become the friends we find time to see when we're not working. Mark was both a friend and a colleague, but things were not like that in his case, for me at least; our working and our personal relationships didn't coalesce. I was extremely fond of him, felt privileged to be with him, found him entertaining and stimulating and endearing, and rarely fretted about his faults. And I admired him enormously as a colleague – usually as my editor – and look back with satisfaction and even with pride at things we did together. But as a colleague I disliked him. He seemed capricious, domineering and instinctively on the side of the Organisation – Thomson Newspapers or Condé Nast – and almost in opposition to his fellow-workers.

But of course he was a remarkably effective and original editor. It looks as if in retrospect that side of his creative achievement has come to be slightly forgotten as appreciation of his work as a cartoonist has increased. The fact is that it was he personally who showed how to transform photomagazines from penny plain to tuppence coloured. And the colour magazine as a genre was as important a manifestation of the popular culture of the sixties – even if it took time to get beyond the middle class to the masses – as, say, the Beatles. This is not to claim that its impact was due to Mark's personal brilliance: there were so many economic and technological factors working in its favour that it could scarcely have failed to take. But it was Mark who gave it its shape. He did so through a wonderful instinct for relating words to images. He had editorial imagination, the power to see what subjects could be treated in his medium, what subjects people could be made to want to know about right now and how those subjects could be treated to advantage. I can illustrate this talent by citing something that happened one day long after he had handed over editorship of the mag to do other jobs for Thomson's.

His successor, Godfrey Smith, besides being a great pleasure to work for, was a very fine editor, widely informed and a sharp spotter of new writers. Mark often joined us at the editorial staff's regular 'ideas meetings'. At one of these, Godfrey suddenly suggested that I should edit a special number on the subject of genius. I was so embarrassed to be linked with such a corny idea that I sat there like a lump of dough. Mark broke into the silence: 'What about doing an issue on the Stein family?', recalling the old limerick:

A terrible family is Stein,
There's Gert and there's Ep and there's Ein.
Gert's poetry is bunk,
Ep's sculpture is junk
And nobody understands Ein.

'Fabulous,' I said. 'We'll also have Wittgenstein and Eisenstein and Trotsky, who was Bronstein, and Roy Lichtenstein, and all those musicians, and then there have even been great Steins in sports management, like Abe Saperstein and Colin Stein. Yes, I'd love to do the Steins.'

To find a specific form for a topic, a concrete embodiment of a vague idea, an embodiment that's both unexpected and inevitable — this is what makes a great editor.

Don't you think your imitation of Twiggy's Evzone-look might be construed in the crescent as sympathy for the Greek junta?

I had to cheer myself up somehow; Tristram has brought home a highly disturbing school report.

See, Joanna. Alpha in Revolutionary Studies and the Marcuse Memorial Prize for Under Tens. So couldn't I go straight up to the Anti-University?

No, Tristram; not while they say "your mind seems elswhere" in Sexual Education periods.

The Public Schools Commission have a point. Fond as we are of Tristram on alternate Saturdays, he's a true case of "boarding need".

It's the key dilemma of the Seventies. As a socialist I abominate the public schools; but as TV executive I believe in revolution from within. So perhaps one could just allow the State to pay for Tristram at Winchester.

Joanna, a photographer is coming round this morning to take some pictures to publicise my TV show. As it's my last day under your roof I wonder if I could borrow Simon's caftan?

Yes, Simon isn't wearing it since the Arab/Israeli war: he doesn't want people to suspect him of pro-Arab sympathies.

Joanna, do you think I should ask the photographer to lunch?

The answer is 'Yes' if he's a cockney making his way up; but if it turns out to be Lord Snowdon, you should recommend the nearest pub.

While we're waiting for our photographer to show, Mr Goldblatt, I wonder if we could gather some caption-fodder?

I'm planning a Christmas production of 'Winnie the Pooh'. But the really original idea is to do it in the correct dress of the period.

Meriel McCooey

The *Sunday Times* magazine first appeared in 1962. It was a disaster. The dummy which had been produced by John Anstey, later the editor of the *Telegraph* magazine was bad enough, full of shiny cars and nubile model girls. Then, CD (later Sir Denis) Hamilton, the *Sunday Times* Editor, realising that it was an absolute lulu recruited Mark Boxer from the 'trendy' *Queen* magazine where he was art editor. Together he and Gordon Moore produced the first issue, a publication that was grey, uninteresting, lacking in ideas and direction. Other journalists relieved, overjoyed perhaps, dubbed it boring, uncompetitive and boasted it was the first item they trashed every Sunday. This smug dismissal didn't last long. Mark recruited Michael Rand as art editor from the *Express*, poached Francis Wyndham from *Queen* where they had worked together and drew up a distinguished list of contributors, who like Mark were talented, enthusiastic and imaginative. He employed artists like Peter Blake and David Hockney, photographers Cartier-Bresson, David Montgomery and Don McCullin, top-notch writers like Angus Wilson, John Mortimer and Robert Kee, and art specialist David Sylvester. When I joined the paper a couple of years later, I was employed as one of the Women's Editor Ernestine Carter's 'gels' to write about such things as oyster cream and corsets. Luckily for me, Mark and Ernestine were neither glamoured nor frightened by each other, just wary. After a few attempts to gain complete control over the fashion pages in the magazine, Ernestine reluctantly delegated the job to me, thus ending their mutual culture crisis – 'She writes for the trade,' Mark would snap. I was still on Ernestine's budget though I changed desks to one on the magazine two floors below. Mark was money conscious, often paying talented people like Don McCullin peanuts, but he was generous with his own flair – though simultaneously making life a misery for those who didn't live up to his high standards. Someone once remarked that 'he didn't suffer fools gladly'. Truthfully, he didn't suffer them at all.

His magazine epitomised the sixties and mirrored the observable realities of what was going on in the world, and it began to work because he was excellent at writing qualitative gossip, and realising that a publication should be informative, educative and entertaining.

He could be serious as well as mischievous, enthusiastic, wonderfully stylish, often mysterious. Once he confessed he had been in repertory and had played maids turned into butlers. I had spent some time with various rep companies

playing butlers turned into maids. But he never revealed where he had been a thespian or what had attracted him to journalism.

He was friendly with (Lord) Snowdon and introduced him to CD who immediately put him on the staff. Mark suggested that I should work with Peter Knapp, who was the art director, *éminence grise* of *Elle* magazine and a brilliant fashion photographer. He utilised the talents of Robert Freson, but didn't ignore those of the British brigade of Bailey, Duffy and Donovan. In fact Bailey's *Book of Pin-ups* with words by Francis has become a collector's item.

When Mark, Michael and Francis got together they almost always produced something profoundly provocative. Francis's article on P. J. Proby probably almost gave CD a heart attack. Poor chap, he liked the sort of features we nicknamed 'Wholly Delightfuls'. These were articles and pictures that never attracted a letter, critical or otherwise, had little journalistic merit and usually were accompanied by photographs of glorious sunsets. 'Oh he's just being a bit of a fuddy-duddy,' Mark would say dismissively of CD's gentlemanly but anguished criticisms.

He loved games and about 6 p.m. would sometimes sit down with Francis, David Sylvester, Suzanne Hodgart, myself and whoever else happened to be around to play bridge. Though he was passionate about the game he lacked the Machiavellian skills of David and Francis. He was equally fond of cricket. Once, when he broke his drawing finger playing, he was delighted when the doctor asked him his age and said 'but I thought you were much, much younger'. Mark's pleasure was quite poignant. He kept repeating the story to everyone. I had no idea he cared about age and aging.

Like most creative people Mark had a bleak side, with a personal life messed up by his romantic expectations. Once booking a table for lunch from a phone in the middle of the office, we overheard him talking to the booker at Chez Victor saying, 'Can I book a bed for two – oops I mean table,' but laughed when he realised we were listening.

I saw very little of him when he moved to Weidenfeld's and nothing after he went to Condé Nast. But those who knew him well missed his vitality and his ability to trim, tailor and often improve on ideas. Often he was wrong but this never inhibited his animated zeal for a good feature. If he noticed a glazed look in some-one's eyes as he explained an idea, he would grab a scrap of paper and draw it out for them.

Eventually, in 1965 his interest in the magazine waned and he left to start *London Life*, taking with him Francis, and David Hillman from the art department, and persuaded David Putnam to join them. *London Life* was a flop. It was *Time Out* at the wrong time. Just nine months later they all began to drift back, Mark as an assistant editor on the paper and cartoonist on *The Times*, Francis to the magazine, though David Hillman joined Pentagram and David Putnam went into film production. Godfrey Smith became editor of the magazine but he always asked Mark to our weekly meetings and usually referred to him as 'the young master'.

In an introduction to one of her books, Mark's first wife Arabella wrote: 'Now that my husband and children have grown up and left home…' 'But I don't think he ever did,' said a close friend.

‘What about a car sticker, Ma'am, saying 'Don't blame us, we voted Labour'?,

‘I want to sell my Telecom shares, but I can't get through,

‘He really must fancy me — I'm not on expenses...,

‘And if they do turn out to be fake, we can always enter them for the Booker Prize,

George Melly

Even now, reading the papers in bed, I automatically make a mental note of those subjects likely to spark off a pocket-cartoon later that morning and sometimes there is a *donnée*, complete with captions, which I know would have stimulated Mark's involuntary irresistible giggle, and signalled that our daily chore was over.

I'd known him long before our collaboration and we were already friends but, through working with him, I really got to understand his qualities and defects, and learnt to accept those occasional explosions of bad temper, knowing they would be immediately replaced by an apology as warm and reassuring as a spontaneous hug. Through 'Marc' I learnt to love Mark.

It was not just our very different physical appearances (Falstaff and Prince Hal) which slightly intimidated me, although I think, combined with his inability to make a clumsy gesture, this certainly came into it. More to the point was his unconscious ability to impose the idea that he was the definitive mould of fashion and the glass of form, a figure of urbane sophistication all the more convincing for being understated. His approval therefore solicited a puppy-like fawning on my part which I regretted but was unable to do anything about.

There were however areas where his inability to question his infallibility was less convincing. In particular his scornful indifference to anywhere north of Hampstead, let alone Watford, was a constant irritant. Nor could he believe that anyone could fail to share his enthusiasm for cricket, or be genuinely obsessed by fishing. This was the cause of some friction between us. If he intended to go to Lord's he would change the time of our daily telephone call without any hesitation, whereas if I wanted to spend a morning by the river he could become quite tetchy.

Above all he was totally at a loss to explain my decision in the early seventies, to return to jazz-singing, especially as it involved touring the provinces. My assurance that I actually enjoyed it he dismissed as making a virtue out of a necessity and, in the kindest possible spirit, he offered insistently to approach people to set me up in a club as host *à la* Nell's in New York. I could even sing now and then he assured me doubtfully. The thing was he never understood that I love singing, nor could he take aboard that I would no longer enjoy staying up each night into the small hours.

Our taste in painting was another point of friction. What he liked in general was a certain aesthetic abstraction, rather pale in colour and unalarmingly discreet. When we first met he was openly dismissive of my passion for Magritte, a view

'I hear our manager's putting his wife on the transfer list,'

'Perhaps the Queen should abdicate in _her_ favour...'

'Arthur's also sent a protest to Gadafy — for pushing the miners off the front page,'

'Now she seems to be competing with the Prince of Wales,'

admittedly shared by most informed opinion, but later, when Magritte became acceptable, he cleverly modified his opinion. 'I always think,' he said, well aware that I owned, at that time, several originals, 'that he looks so much better in reproduction.' If I wrote a piece for him the same applied. Anything outside his terms of reference was edited out, for he concluded that if he didn't get the point no one else would either. He was probably right, but it was still, I thought, a shade cavalier.

He applied roughly the same criteria when it came to the cartoons, but here I felt he was justified. He understood, and could pin down with a devastating accuracy, the Sloanes, the rich bitches, the 'great and the good', the arrogant upper classes, the self-regarding creatures of the media, vain and silly actors, corseted or cloned queens, international white trash, lion-hunting hostesses, reactionary clubmen, and smug liberals. On the other hand he was weak on the drabber suburbs, the working class and, predictably, the provinces. I tended therefore to skirt these areas but sometimes, during the miners' strike for instance, they were unavoidable. Mark, if the idea was strong enough, did his best, but his miners were not too convincing. Still partial to anachronistic cloth caps, they somehow gave the impression of responding to some whim of the fashion industry in favour of proletarian chic. On his own turf however he was unequalled and, if I'd contributed to an idea I knew to be spot on, I would long to see how he had interpreted or, to be more accurate, transformed it. He was quite brilliant at exploiting the simplest devices: a pair of earrings, a way of sitting on a bar stool, a dinner-table setting, to imply a complete social attitude.

If I have given the impression that all the ideas were mine I must correct it. Sometimes he would already have thought of one when I rang up, and here he would show a considerable sensitivity. 'Perhaps,' he'd suggest, 'you could sharpen up the caption.' Quite often too neither of us would have come up with anything in advance, and would volley the day's events back and forth until we reached a mutually agreeable solution. He would however never accept a sub-standard notion. 'It doesn't make me laugh,' he'd say wearily, and just once or twice he'd abandon the task altogether rather than submit a cartoon below his own inflexible standard.

He was not only a beady-eyed social commentator, but a fastidious draftsman. The end-product may look effortless, but even the pocket-cartoons were often redrawn several times until he was quite satisfied they were 'right', while his more ambitious caricatures (his method was to modify and perfect them through many sheets of tracing paper) were not only excellent physical likenesses but, at the same time, exposed the pretensions of his victims with merciless accuracy. He once showed me a long list of those he hoped to get around to eventually. Judging by the enraged reaction of some of those he'd already tackled, they should be relieved that his untimely death allowed them to remain as future projects only.

He had a unique mannerism. Often, contrary to the usual practice of caricaturists, he would treat the head with delicate subtlety, and dash in the clothes with apparently clumsy brushstrokes. Yet this method worked triumphantly well. His subjects emerged like absurd moths from their sartorial cocoons. Mark thought of his drawing, not as a footnote to a busy and largely successful career, but as his most important contribution. Personally I believe he was right to do so.

I began to work with Mark in the late sixties and continued until shortly before his death. It was an indication of his realistic perception that his main focus moved gradually towards the right. While himself a left-wing sympathiser, a fact which may surprise those who knew him only as a social figure, his principal subject was always bad faith, and although his well-heeled media liberals were still there under Thatcher, they rapidly lost ground as the mouthpiece of received opinion. In consequence his dinner parties shifted from N.W.1 to S.W.1. Uneasy conscience yielded to defiant spending, the Norland nanny replaced the au pair, the voice of the Stringalongs was no longer heard (or at any rate heeded) in the land. Sex, however, remained a constant even if its setting implied Colefax and Fowler rather than Habitat. Like a Restoration playwright, Mark realised that nothing reveals our vanities, our self-delusions and cynical manipulation of others better than what we get up to in, or en route to, bed.

Sometimes this landed him in hot water, but then so did our shared mistrust of received religion, jokes about the Royals, and especially ideas offensive to the ethics of the newspaper by whom we were currently employed. When he felt that his freedom to satirise a subject he felt deserved it, was under threat, he resigned rather than compromise. To have succeeded in quitting both the *Guardian* and *The Times* on these grounds was not only a remarkable achievement but a proof of his obstinate integrity. Strangely enough the *Telegraph*, his final home, proved the least censorious, but then perhaps his death forestalled an eventual showdown.

In general, however, his pocket-cartoons were cherished, whereas his single caricatures could cause real offence, and especially a series of prominent London hostesses which appeared in the *Tatler* under his editorship. Objectively it is easy to understand why. Not only were they physically the reverse of charitable, but they revealed, with the precision of an expert lobotomist, the social pretensions and, where applicable, sexual propensities of his victims. Mark never understood the pain and fury they aroused. He felt that if a drawing was both funny and accurate that was its only necessary justification. He once told me that one of his subjects had threatened to have his legs broken. He seemed genuinely puzzled, but as the drawing implied insatiable nymphomania, I was considerably less mystified. It was a curious blind spot.

Mark's courage really came into its own when his brain tumour was diagnosed. I went to see him in hospital in the early stages, and he was at his funniest. He told me on that visit that he intended to continue to draw his cartoons as long as he was able to, and so he did, although it became increasingly difficult as his mind began to break up. In the end I would dictate an idea to Anna in the hope it would replace the caption in an earlier drawing, but eventually it reached a point where nothing 'made him laugh' because he could no longer grasp even the simplest idea. He remained, however, very sweet-natured, unaffected by his loss of looks (and he was not without vanity in that direction) and apparently able to accept the inevitable without fear or anger.

The last time I saw him was in his garden. He knew who I was, but complained mildly that the three thousand pounds' worth of plants that he'd ordered had failed to be delivered. He drifted in and out of sleep, impervious to his children noisily at play. He died ten days later.

In a piece I wrote about him for the *Tatler* shortly afterwards I said that the immediate effect of his death was a kind of anger at its arbitrary unfairness. Mark was to do with life.

This feeling has of course faded, although the memory of his physical grace, his wit and relish for absurdity, remains undiminished. I can still visualise him exactly and hear his voice.

Recently I had a dream about him. I was following him round a suite of offices, presumably those of a glossy magazine of which he was editor. I was trying to think of an idea for a cartoon but it was very difficult, not only because he was so busy checking layouts, making decisions, and so on, but because I knew he was dead. In the end I challenged him with it, 'Of course I died,' he said impatiently, 'but I decided to come back.' I told him that I didn't know this was possible. 'Anybody can do it,' he explained, 'but most people prefer it on the other side, in fact everybody does, but I didn't.'

It seemed, in his case, absolutely reasonable. I understood at once.

Vicki Woods

I realised Mark's power over women after he'd been at *Tatler* about a week. In late 1984, the women at Vogue House were starting to power-dress, after the prevailing fashion, and to wear shoulder pads inside their jackets, which were made of rather masculine fine tweed. Their skirts were snugly fitted and beginning to rise above the knee. I'd been going over headlines with Mark in his little office and we gathered up all the layouts to take back into the art-room. Gliding along the corridor towards us came the managing editor Christina Garrett in a real humdinger of a suit: artfully cut in tiny checks of black and white. Mark, who was long-leggedly striding ahead of me, stopped dead, smiled at her, tucked his left hand into his pocket and stuck his right arm out to lean against the wall, the long diagonal of his body therefore barring her way. Chris was brought up short and reared back on her heels a bit so as not to actually brush bosoms with him. Mark looked down from his great height. 'Wonderful suit,' he said. 'Who's your tailor?' Chris opened her mouth to answer, but she was ducking down slightly at the same time in order to pass under the arch of his arm. 'Ah –' she said breathily. I thought for a second it was an involuntary moan brought on by intense sexual feeling as in a Kim Basinger movie – 'Aaah ...' It could have been, but it wasn't. The slight breathlessness was engendered by the arm-block and the ducking-down, but she was actually telling him the name of her tailor. 'Armani.' He made an 'I'm impressed' face and let her go. Putty in his hands.

He was so clearly the handsomest man in the history of the world that even the very young women at *Tatler* – chippy twentysomethings who lived by different sexual mores (modern; bleaker) and hated the dandiness of his more elderly suits ('Ach – *flares*. Ugh – *kipper ties*') – would gaze at old Snowdon pictures of him at the height of his startling beauty and say, 'Oh all right, I grant you; he was very handsome. In the *seventies*.'

But his charm would melt even these hard young women when he turned it on them. He was a Beauty in the way that a woman is a Beauty, and he had all the easy charm and power that beauty brings. *Tatler* did a big feature on beauties, new and old, and I had to spend weeks gazing at hundreds of pictures of luminescent women, beauties of the sixties, of the seventies, current young beauties of the mid-eighties and I became crosser and crosser writing headlines and standfirsts and pull-quotes for these pictures, and finding scraps of verse and bits out of Zuleika Dobson to describe these flowers of my sex. I burst out: 'God, I'd give ANYTHING

44

'He took me to this glam place and then he told me he was doing a feature about being a mistress,

'The trouble with the modern office party is that there's nothing big enough to take the typist behind,

'I've run out of fags, so I'll just nip round to the Palace,

'I was terribly worried that Charles was involved with a takeover bid, but thank heavens it's only a topless model, for beauty! Anything I have, I'd swap! Brains, wit, money, happiness … anything.'

Mark put on a deeply concerned face, shaking his head. 'No, no, no, darling, you wouldn't.' 'Oh, but I would, most certainly I would.' 'No, darling, absolutely, I promise you, you wouldn't.' 'Well, why wouldn't I, in heaven's name?' 'Because beauty fades,' he said. 'For women, it fades. If you did have beauty, it would go, inevitably, and you'd lose your looks and all your power and you'd become distraught, like so many women, wonderful-looking women, when they get to forty and it disappears, and they look in the mirror and can't cope and everything that was easy for them when they were young and had beauty becomes so hard and hopeless. Believe me (eyes looking fixedly at me in an earnest, meeting gaze) you're MUCH, much better as you are.'

I went to dinner at Christ Church a couple of months before I left *Tatler* in 1987. The men, like the wines, were deep and full-bodied and powerful; and the women, like the endless courses of food, were badly presented, chilly and dull. They didn't talk much; just sat between the dons like heaps of compost. One of the heaps suddenly said in a carrying voice, 'Did I hear you say you worked for *Tatler*?' 'Well, yes, I do,' I said, rather defiantly. It seemed a flibbertigibbet vocation in this heavyweight company. 'Does … Mark Boxer still edit that?' she said, and I guessed why she was asking. She was over fifty, and quite pleasant-looking; a bit hefty about the body and wispy about the hair and abstractedly dressed in the North Oxford fashion. 'Did you know him at Cambridge?' I said. She blushed, looked away and started fiddling with her butter-knife. 'Well, he wouldn't remember ME, of course; wouldn't remember my name: probably – he was – *lots* of us, we all – rather beneath his notice, you know…'

'Was he terribly, terribly beautiful at Cambridge?' I asked her, and she just said 'Oh!' and then she said 'Oh!' again, but then she suddenly burst out, very theatrical: 'He Walked Among Us Like A God.' I promise that's what she said and with that delivery. It might have been irony, but I didn't see any.

I waited until Mark was surrounded inescapably by as many *Tatler* staff as I could manage – about ten of us at the local Chinese restaurant for (I think) Jonathan Meades's leaving lunch. I said: 'I met somebody at Christ Church who knew you, Mark.'

He was as vain as a two-year-old. 'Oh, really, who?'

'She said you wouldn't remember her name. She remembered you vividly from Cambridge.'

'Oh, ye-es?'

'Yes. You obviously made a huge impression on her; she talked of nothing else at dinner.'

'Oh, ye-es?'

By this time, enough slightly oiled people were listening in. I said in a carrying voice, 'This is what she said at high table: "He Walked Among Us Like A God."' The whole lunch-party shouted with scornful delight and Mark, giggling like a maniac, sat bending his knees up to his chin in *faux*-modesty: 'Oh, stop it, Vicki, she can't have; no, really, it's too much.' And waited for me to go on.

He taught me a lot. The first piece I wrote for him was about an amazingly vulgar but rather clever advertising man. I followed him around for a day, while he held meetings and showed off and, at Mark's urging, wrote a piece that laid about me right and left. One paragraph he specially liked. I said that I'd pressed Mr Advertising's doorbell promptly, at Oh-Eight-Thirty-Five hours exactly, as arranged, and the door had been opened by a cross cleaning-woman in a pinny and pink rubber gloves. I breezily asked her if the master of the house was within, adding that he was expecting me. She led me into the hall and said, 'Wait here, please. I'll go and see.' I roamed around the hall for a few minutes, picking up artefacts and putting them down again in a reporterly manner, until the cleaning-woman came back and caught me and said, 'He's upstairs. Will you follow me, please?' In a vast drawing-room, my interviewee waited, in a tracksuit, and he despatched the cleaning-woman off to fetch herb tea before launching into his first monologue. She came back with the tea. I said abstractedly, 'Yes. Just there. Fine.' 'Mmmm, darling, thank you so much,' said Mr Advertising, giving her a smacking kiss. I reeled in my chair. This was *Mrs* Advertising and I began going over and over what I'd said to her downstairs, wondering whether it indicated that I'd taken her for a cleaning-woman. On balance, I thought it did. On balance, I thought, so did she. Mr Advertising was generally believed to have married somewhat above himself, so it was a telling mistake. I put all this in my piece. Mark sniggered all the way through the paragraph and ticked it with his little India-ink ticks (backward ticks – he was left-handed) before crossing it all out. He said, 'It's very funny, but we can't print it. Below the belt. He's responsible for his own actions, so he's fair game, but he's not responsible for hers. You mustn't ever get at a man through his wife. Nothing's more hurtful.' I've thought of Mark's stricture many times since. Gallantry is unfashionably sexist, but very powerful. I watched Geoffrey Howe accept a *Spectator* Parliamentarian of the Year award in 1991. His speech of thanks was extremely brief but he then launched into an angry defence of his wife Elspeth who had been the subject of a cruel newspaper profile. As I listened, and watched the men shifting about and wishing old Geoffrey would stop wittering on, Mark's voice floated into my head. 'You mustn't ever get at a man through his wife. Nothing's more hurtful.'

Everybody who worked for him or with him learned something about their trade. Willie Landels used to lament that 'nobody could draw the upper classes like Marc'. ('Crinkled hair,' Mark told me. 'Look at Prince Charles.') His casual remarks about human frailty – and about journalism, which is pretty much the same thing – floated on after him and became received wisdom; not particularly because the things he said were wiser or cleverer than anyone else's *pensées*, but because he handed you his. Whenever two or three of Mark's ex-*Tatler* people are gathered together, somebody will float up a 'Mark always said', as: 'The thing with secrets is that everybody always tells one person. So when you tell a secret, you have to know who they'll tell.' 'The problem with gossip columnists is that to be good they have to fink on their friends.' 'Write it NOW: nobody can remember anything after two years.' 'The back page should always be funny.' Every time I hold a meeting at *Harpers & Queen* I look round and think *too many damn people at this meeting.* Sometimes I even say it, and they look at me, baffled, not knowing that Mark always said that a meeting should never be more than six people.

48

‘Bright chap, but we don't have to promote him — luckily he's white,

‘He's down... he's out... It's tennis ... No, it's cricket...,

‘Hey kids, would you turn down your Madonna record — your mother can't hear her Elvis Presley's,

‘Sandra now rings up her press agent to pretend she's _not_ going out with Prince Andrew...,

Martin Amis

Not long after Mark's death Anna Ford came to dinner – and gave me one of his neckties. I was pleased, touched and, I remember, physically flattered. The next day I seized my new tie and put it on. And it looked ridiculous. It was of another scale entirely. It looked like a Miss World sash. Mark was, of course, much taller than me, but the disparity was not to do with size alone. It was to do with a personal opulence that was his and not mine. At a lunch, long ago, I asked the company to choose sides between F. R. Leavis and Bloomsbury – to say which world they would have gravitated to, back then: Bloomsbury or Leavisland. Everyone except me chose Bloomsbury. But only Mark gave – only Mark could give – that quietly scandalised whinny of incredulity: it wouldn't cross his mind that there was any real choice in the matter. When thinking about Mark one must immediately cast off the crabbed, the gingerly, the inhibited – the Leavisite, in a word. He was what Darwinians would call a genetic celebrity. He was prodigious; his looks, his life-glow, filled the room; he was almost embarrassingly handsome, but unremote. Once your embarrassment had been mastered, he was a pleasure to be near. When I dream about him I wake up still smelling the aroma of his presence.

In a typical dream I confront him on a street at dusk or in the hallway of a restaurant or in some spectral gathering in a panelled room. I say, 'Mark! You're still alive!' He looks at me with humorous intimacy and says something like: 'I know. It's a secret. Anna has been staying at Arnold Schwarzenegger's house. The children go by plane.' And I say, 'But this is wonderful. That you're still here.' He twinkles at me potently, as if coming back from the dead – or not dying – is a trick available only to the embarrassingly handsome. 'I know,' he agrees. 'But better not tell anyone.' And I promise I won't ... Saul Bellow has said that there is no need to visit the dead, because they are always visiting you.

Still recuperating from my embarrassment, I used to regard Mark snidely when, in his white suit, he used to sweep into the offices of the *Times Literary Supplement*, twenty years ago. I thought it appropriate that he was there to help with the 'look' of the paper where I rather dingily worked as a trainee editorial assistant. The first words I ever addressed to him were: 'Are you taking my pulse?' This was said aggressively at the opening party for a now-vanished magazine (*The New Review*): Mark was lifting my arm out of the way, to clear his path to a woman we were both interested in. He looked at me, then, with patient amusement. I think, in a way, that he *was* taking my pulse. After a while he asked me out to lunch. For some time we were more than acquaintances but we weren't quite friends. There was attraction, and also opposition. The opposition had to do with: rigour v. frivolity, the novel v. the cartoon, the written v. the visual, the slob v. the dandy, the pubgoer v. the socialite, 5′ 6″ v. 6′ 2″. Leavisland v. Bloomsbury.

Our friendship solidified over the chessboard. Mark would produce his set at the lunch-table, or in cocktail bars (he would enter a pub only as a last resort: he looked like some duchess visiting the East End), or in my impeccably Leavisite flat in Queensway, where he would come increasingly often in the early evenings, two, three, four times a week. When playing White he typically favoured the King's Gambit. After 1. P-K4 P-K4, White offers the pawn sacrifice with 2. P-KB4. The idea is to castle early and make dashing attacks down the cleared King's Bishop file. This opening is now discredited (so far as I can see White has no hope of castling after 3. ... B-K2), but Mark had many racy successes with it. Our results were very even; the difference in our styles was diametrical. Mark was the insouciant trader in lyrical combinations, I the dour counterpuncher and percentage man. He thought it a humiliation not to get things wrapped up by the late middle game. Thereafter he grew bored and careless. If you got to the end game on level terms, you had won. While we played, Mark would have a drink, or he wouldn't have a drink. He would smoke a cigarette or he wouldn't smoke a cigarette. He could smoke one cigarette, or ten cigarettes, or no cigarettes. He was not an addictive personality. I was, and am. In terms of spirit and manner, I was always playing Black. Mark was always playing White.

In the late seventies Mark published a full-page caricature of me so insulting that I thought the least I could do was never speak to him again. The truth was I didn't mind *that* much; but it would have seemed feeble, or even masochistic, to do otherwise, such was the detailed hostility contained in that drawing. It was easily the most violent cartoon he ever presented to the public eye (in comparison, he never laid a glove on Lord Longford or Georgie Best); and Marc was known, not for his violence, but for his quiet elegance and cleanness of line. I was depicted, in any event, at shin-height to a gathering of women whose dresses I was supposed to be peering up — overweight, with terrible hair, and a penis instead of a nose. The caption went something like: Amo, Amis, Amat, Amaravis, Amarartist, Amarunt. To common friends Mark was saying that he didn't know what had come over him. But *I* knew, I think. All interesting friendships, like marriages, are built on an argument, or a contrast. And they are love—hate: amo, amis, amat. Mark's drawing was his side of the argument, and an assertion of his artistic independence. It was also an example of his complex and compulsive urge to be honest (he was a brickdropper in the grand manner, on a par with Gielgud). After a year or so the offence seemed to be purged. I called him; we had a game of chess. The friendship resumed, and intensified.

His honesty, his candour, stemmed from a wonderful confidence in his own instincts. He did want to hear about your troubles and was instantly and intelligently sympathetic. As I remember, his advice was always very clear and straightforward; and it was always based on the pleasure principle. Do the things that are likely to bring you pleasure. He was undevious, untortured. We were all not guilty – was his view. He never blamed anyone for anything. He was just not interested in assigning blame. When he was dying he assigned no blame, metaphysical or otherwise. 'I don't mind dying,' he said to me, in the hospital. Or again: 'I don't mind being dead.' For Anna and the girls he minded beyond words; but not for himself. His equanimity during those last weeks seemed to me extraordinary at the time – and even more extraordinary now. In life his manner and presence were always soft and fond; when he was dying he became infinitely gentle.

I remember – and will never forget – the last time I visited him. I had come to say goodbye: the next day I was going with my family to America, and both Mark and I knew that we would never see each other again (though it felt like quite a while before I got the inevitable telephone call and, a day or two later, found myself sitting on a porch reading his obituary in the *New York Times*). I parked the car in the street outside, and looked up. It might have been accumulated dread, or pathetic fallacy, but the pretty house seemed to have an absolutely terrible colour: bruised and swelling and thunderous. I rang the bell. Only the housekeeper was home: she greeted me with a horrified look and said I couldn't possibly go up. I persisted. And up I went.

For many, many days he had been getting lower in the bed. Now he was fully horizontal. Usually I would lie there beside him; but the room was flooded with a new darkness and difficulty. I sat facing him and we talked for a few minutes. I kissed him goodbye and as I stood up I said, 'You have all my thoughts.' He paused and then said clearly, 'And you have mine.' I was master of myself as I took leave of the house. I felt in quiet control as I walked down the street to the car. The instant I shut the door behind me I started crying as I had not cried for thirty years: childishly, with no possibility of restraint. This went on for some time. As I fumbled for paper tissues I became aware of the passers-by. I felt embarrassed – but I soon got over that. I decided that those who walked that street, that summer, must have grown accustomed to seeing people crying in cars.

The portraits

George Brown

Marc

Huw Weldon

Marc

Solly Zuckerman

Selwyn Lloyd

Marc

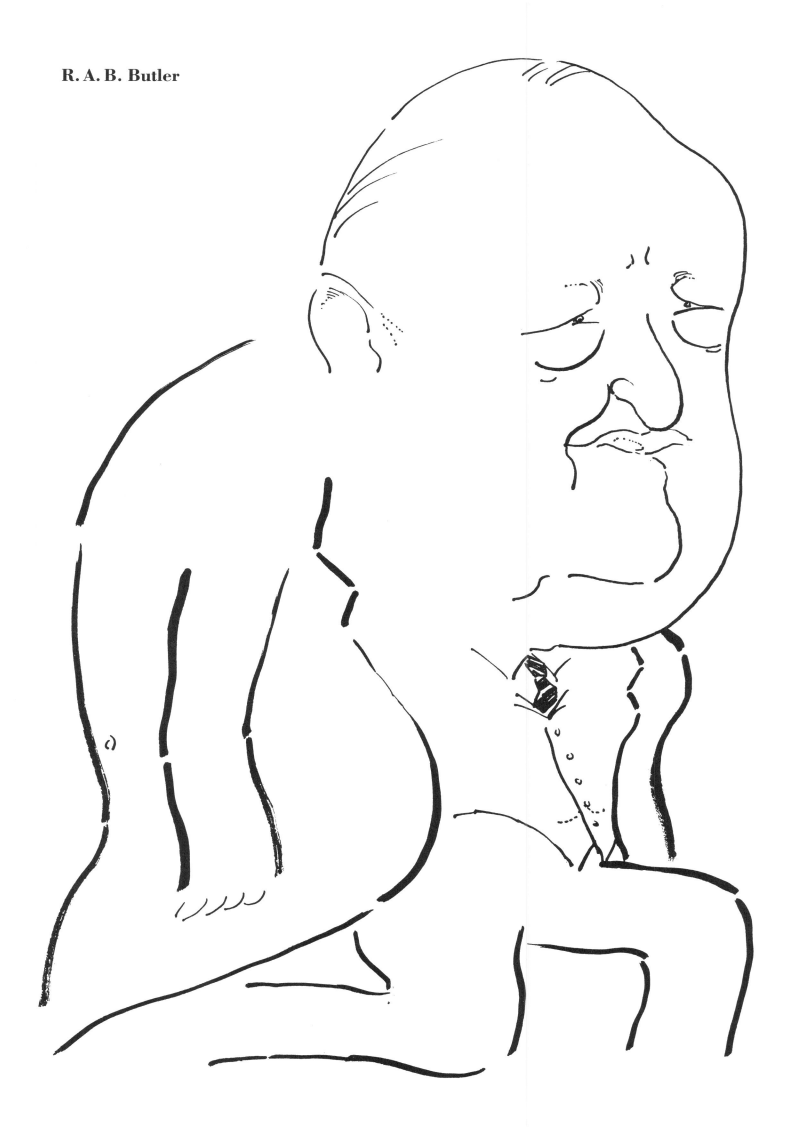

R. A. B. Butler

Clive Jenkins

Malcolm Muggeridge

Arnold Goodman

Harold Macmillan

YOU'VE NEVER HAD IT SO GOOD

HER MAJESTI

Alec Douglas-Home

Marcia Falkender
& Harold Wilson

Ted Heath

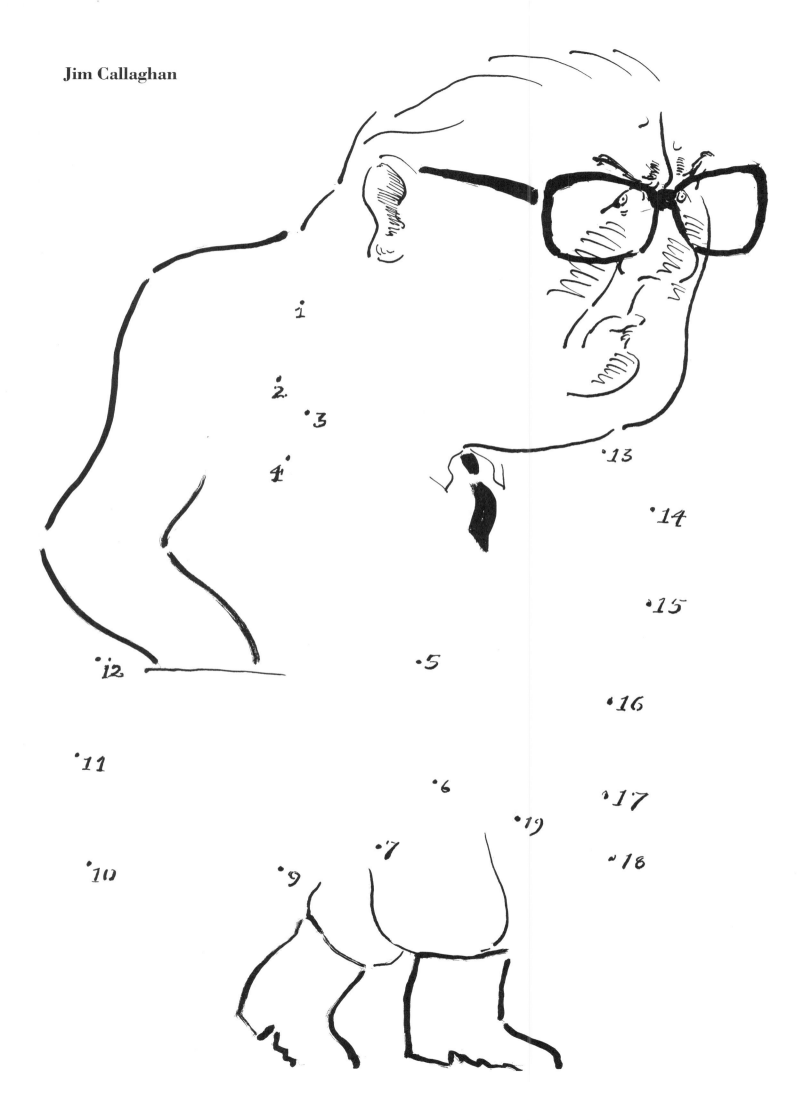

Jim Callaghan

Margaret Thatcher

Marc

Paul Foot

THE TIMES

Times Newspapers Limited, P.O. Box no. 7, New Printing House Square,
Gray's Inn Road, London WC1X 8EZ (registered office)
Telephone 01-837 1234 Telex 264971 Registered no. 894646 England

Roy Thomson

Rupert Murdoch

Shirley Williams

Jeremy Thorpe

Denis Healey

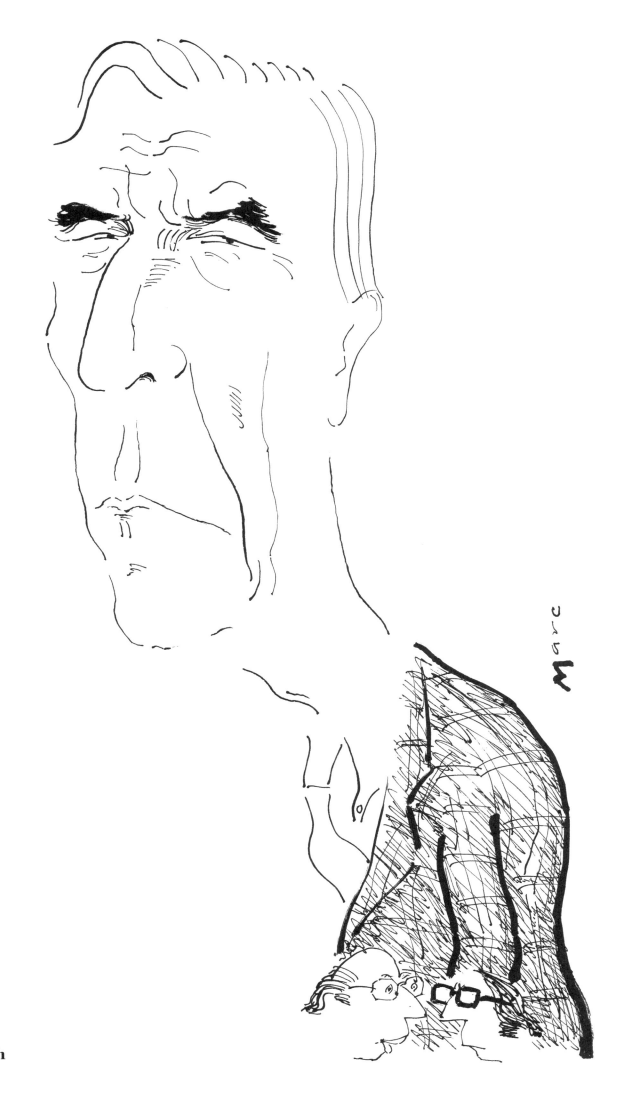

J. K. Galbraith

F. R. Leavis

Marc

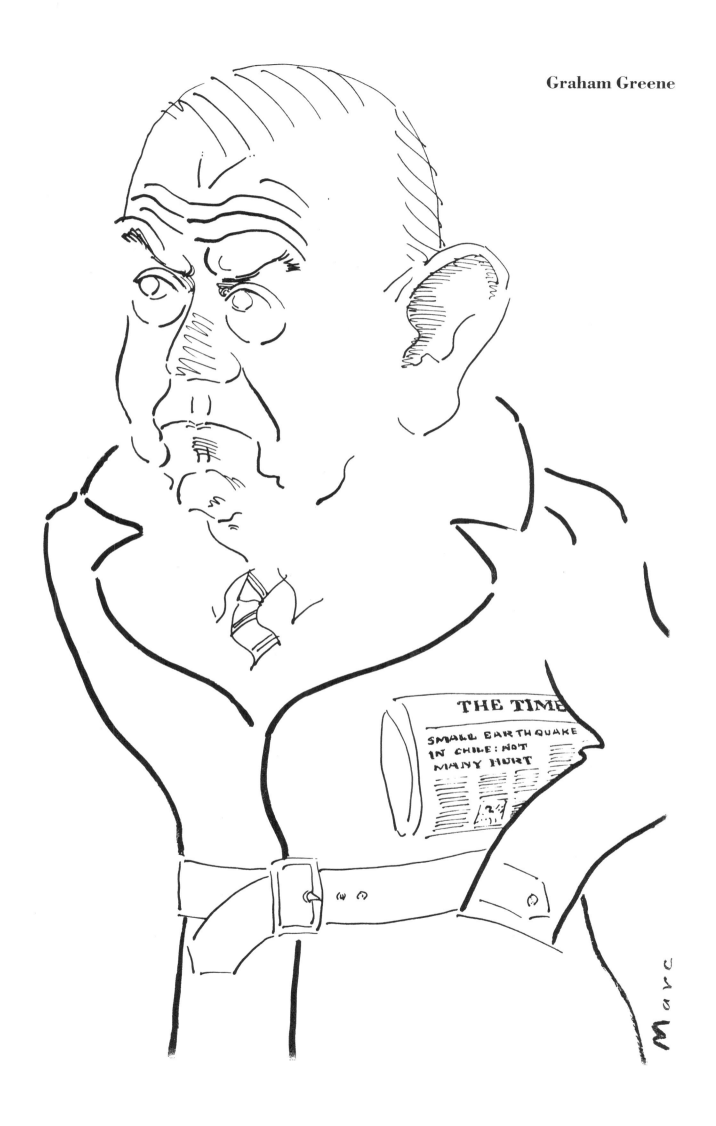

Graham Greene

THE TIME

SMALL EARTHQUAKE
IN CHILE: NOT
MANY HURT

Marc

Prince Edward

Alan Whicker

Kenneth Tynan & Laurence Olivier

IAGO TEMPTS LORD OTHELLO OF BRIGHTON WITH
A LEWD PLAY BY A PERUVIAN MARXIST

Michael Parkinson

Hardy Amies

Jimmy Hill

Marc

André Previn

Clive Lloyd

John Betjeman

Philip Roth

Mel Brooks

Harold Hobson

Marc

V. S. Naipaul

Martin Amis

Amo, Amis, Amat, Amoramus,
Amorartist, Amorunt...

Ian McEwan

Marc

Gerald, 6th Duke of Westminster

David Eccles

Margaret, Duchess of Argyll

Antony, Lord Lambton

Marc.

Noël Coward

Marc

Tom Stoppard

Marc

Philip, HRH the Duke of Edinburgh

Cecil Beaton

Germaine Greer

Richard Ingrams

Geoffrey Howe

George Weidenfeld

Marc

Harry Evans

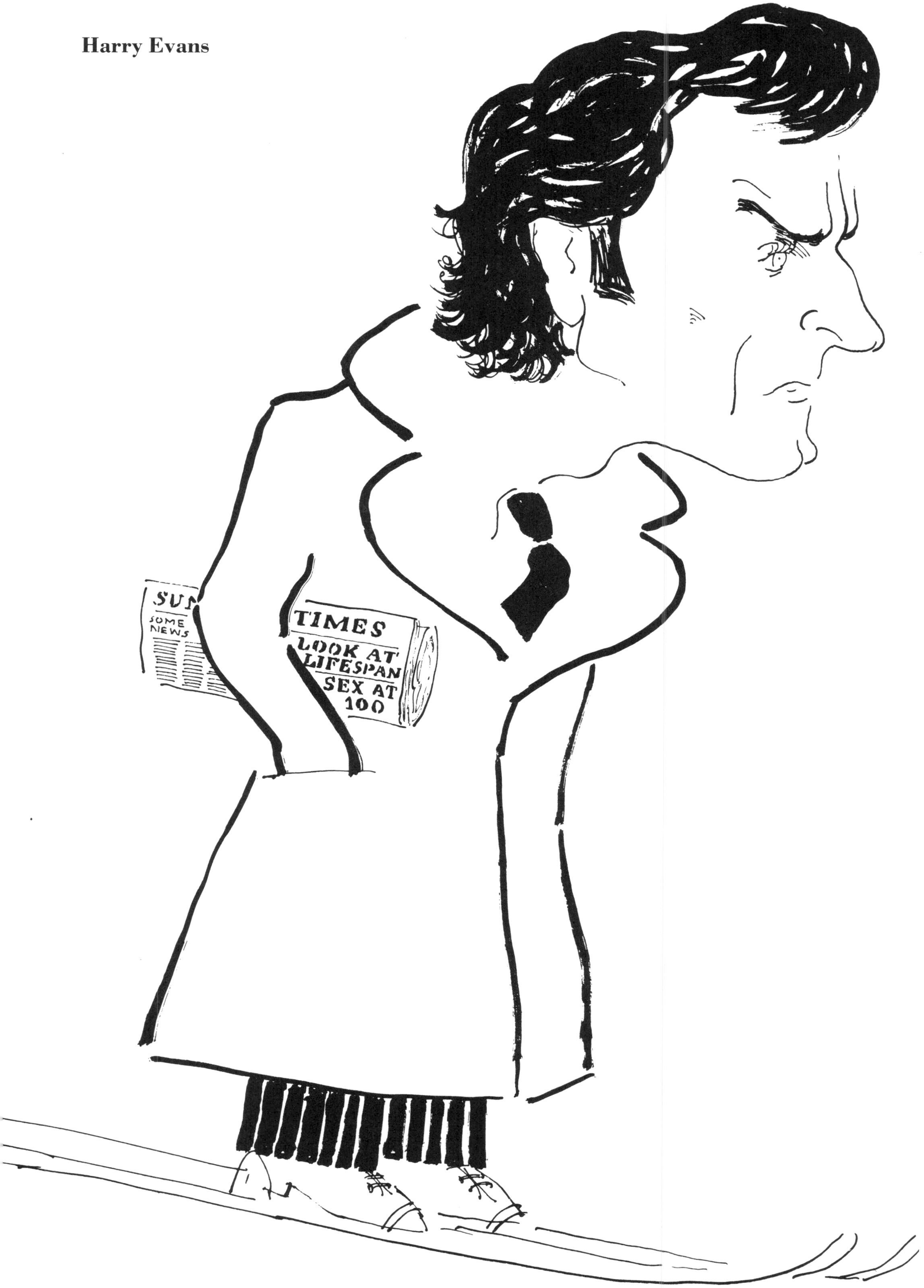
SOME NEWS
TIMES
LOOK AT LIFESPAN
SEX AT 100

Tony Crosland

Marc

C. D. Hamilton

**Bernard Levin
& Clive James**

John Aspinall

Henry Kissinger

Arianna Stassinopoulos

Michael Frayn

Jonathan Miller

Noel Annan

Tom Driberg

Jeffrey Archer

Beryl Bainbridge

Elizabeth Taylor

Stephen Spender

David Niven

Marc

Alfred Brendel

Terence Conran

Dennis Potter

Harold Pinter

Kerry Packer

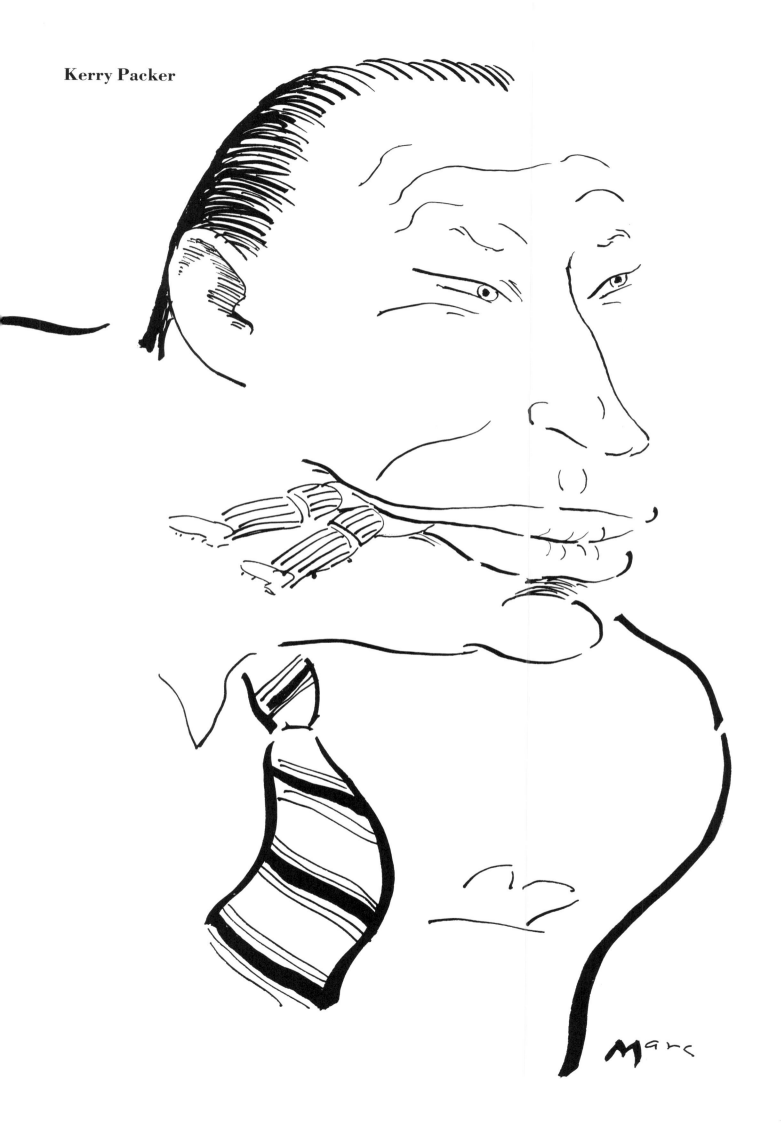

Luis Buñuel

Norman Fowler

Rhodes Boyson

Hugh Trevor-Roper

Lucian Freud

John Gross

Sidney Bernstein

Roy Jenkins

Marc

Leon Brittan

Robin Day

Douglas Hurd

John Biffen

Ian Paisley

Enoch Powell

Marc

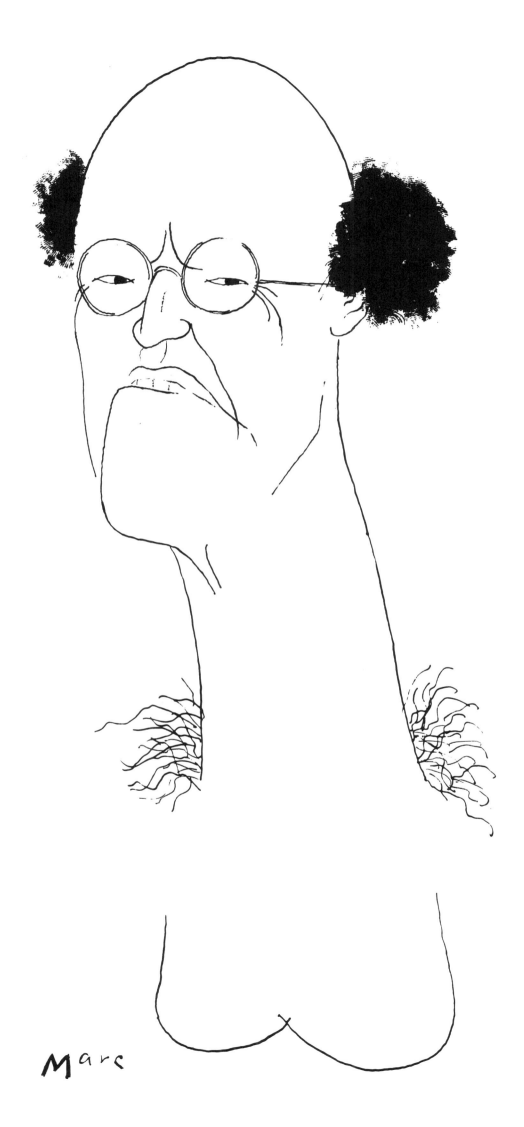

David Owen

Marc

François Mitterrand

"Bubbles"
Rothermere

Henry, 6th Marquess of Bath

Cyril Smith

Marc

Norman St John-Stevas

THIS WAY

Marc

William Rees-Mogg

Andreas Whittam Smith

THE INDEPENDENT

Hugh Fraser

Claus von Bulow

Alastair Burnet

Marc

Angela Rippon

Edward, HRH the 2nd Duke of Kent

Len Murray

Marc

Denis Thatcher

Mark Thatcher

Tony Benn

David Mellor

Marc

Anthony Burgess

John Mortimer

Melvyn Bragg

Alan Bennett

Woodrow Wyatt

David Puttnam

Kurt Vonnegut

Sir Hugh Casson

Gerald Kaufman

Tom King

Marc

Bianca Jagger

David Hockney

Anthony Howard

Kingsley Amis

SPECTATOR

BORING WORDIES
BY PATRICIA
COSGRAVE

Marc

Norman Tebbit

Kenneth Baker

Brian Walden

Willie Whitelaw

A. J. P. Taylor

Arthur Koestler

Marc

Roy Strong